SELECTED POEMS & STORIES
OF CLIFF RHODES - II

by Cliff Rhodes

I0212098

Copyright 2008 by Cliff Rhodes
http://www.lulu.com/sciencefiction
email: rhodesdesigns@yahoo.com

Published at lulu.com

ISBN: 978-0-578-00510-2

For information contact:
Cliff Rhodes
P.O. Box 7095
Meridian, Mississippi 39304-7095

MEMORY IS ANOMALY

What occurs in memory is not what you might think.
We theorize and philosophize but what really happens?
There is no exact occasion that it recovers or goes on the brink.
To be in love or out is not the real concern, even if it saddens.

What we see or imagine is not for real so why all the worry we take,
to bring it back in such great detail as if it should be pristine.
Save the idea of a perfect love, keep it in secret, then let your mind play.
Its colors won't fade or go away, they only grow gray and green.

Stand up for what you believe, in your soul, come rain or shine,
since the weather is quite nice, in the ideal, even on a cloudy day.
No one can take away that beautiful vision since now it is so fine.
Love and liberty are close to the same being, and both are here to stay.

Your memory is not at fault since it is only a vast sea of hearts,
calling for your awakening to come and run to chase the waves.
You cannot catch even one, though you race to find the stars.
Early in the morning they break over you, caressing you with their names.

Here I am now standing in this sea of dreams, knee deep in water,
shivering in the cold and wet and dark, looking far away but not seeing.
Who bids me come to them in this bleak and drab place and does it matter?
You have called me here, so here am I, and no other place do I love being.

It is here where memory lives and none other is better than you,
at making me stay and calling me back from the dark, and the deep blue sea.
Only you would catch away my spirit, and now I fly to see only you could
remain so true,
Is this my curiosity now knocking to open that door of heaven and believe?

Memory is anomaly and requires no belief except in what could be real.
It might be real but is it real, or dream, or vision or both?
You and I know not except what we see in the night, a vision so surreal.
Go now and chase that ocean wave dream like I did and test the waters for
gold.

Tis love, tis gold and you'll know both soon in the memory of one who is new.

*This one you'll not forget nor fail to recall since their name will always
spring true.
Today is the day and never another will reveal such an ocean so blue.
My memory is your memory and both are a watery river that flows, then
goes, so soon.*

by Cliff Rhodes 10/25/2006

SOON AGAIN, TIME WILL BE STEALING

All in one day it came to me
the spirit, the word, the feeling.
We were in pain, all of us,
the pain of rebirth into love.
Never would we pass exactly this way again
since time would see to that and betray.

Stay awhile and wait, just like me.
I'm always here, watching the sea.
It roars in my ears and summons my heart,
reaching into the depths to create art.

Nay, you say there is no art and no love,
yet here they stay, say I, for to live and to run.
The sea will not give up soon its treasure
not a word, not a color, not a pleasure.

Your tongue will not speak, nor eye see,
nor ear ever hear from that deep green.
The sea of reason will not let you rummage
through its boiling waves of watery tonnage.
It gives only what you summon, not request,
from its far flung depths, nothing but its best.

Go now and seek if you will a poem, or pros,
or paint, but can you reach to find even those?
People, many chosen people pass alone through this place
but will not hear even one word, so why give chase?

To seek the knowledge only for to express it
seems trite and self serving but then, why not quit?
Today, it came to you also, the spirit, the word, the feeling.
Soon again you'll be in love, and it too, time will be stealing

by Cliff Rhodes 10/09/2006

4

REALITY OF RECOGNITION

Moving through and into my real eye, the one that realizes,
is this strange phenomenon of enchantment and fascination.
How does it go so smoothly into the waking mind?
The idea takes form and the shape is familiar.
I know this as a friend and the mind takes note.
Does she have form or is she just words and memories?
This is a moment in space and time that is fleeting.
No ghost is this well known, so it is no phantasm.
Waiting for the communication-I look longingly into space.
How long now? Is there some response? Can a memory see?
No, there is no real person-just strings of information and visions.
I don't stop writing, then suddenly-a memory of the moment.
It changes everything and my mind reforms into a new mode.
I'm awake and alert and new things are flashing by.
Thoughts are not communication and never will be.
But what is that reflection that echoes in my mind?
Who put that there? It wasn't me, so how am I thinking,
of this new vision that was not there before? Well,
let's just explain it away and call it recognition.

by Cliff Rhodes 09/19/06

THE SUN, THE MOON, THE DREAM

The sun is up so soon to take away the moon,
and I was hoping that she would stay longer.
My eyes adjust to the light and I think, "Beautiful."
What was that dream I just had and why can't I remember?

Days pass and I reflect what she said or didn't say
even though life goes on and it is so strange that we met.
I am here and she is there in a space that never stays.
What errors have we made in this communication we set?

Have we entombed our minds into this deep green sea
which never can begin to see the light of rule or reason?
How often have we come here to meet in such a dream?
She is often the object of my dream but her face is unseen.

Layers of fantasy and phobia rule the night but soon
there is that quiet place where love is still in bloom.
She takes my hand and we glide together through room
after room of a house so big but neither she nor I can move.

We are frozen, unmoving, and only speak with words of joy
and laughter, even though we stay immobilized and solid.
Soon the light of the sun shines its first rays into our void.
Again we are melted into light and hope and are resolved.

We are determined to find out how next to make this once
and for all merry-go-round of dreams stop its revolving.
Night after night the moon glows and then the sun is upon us.
Then we know, and it occurs that the two are never stopping.
Only we are frozen in time and it is light that is surrounding.

by Cliff Rhodes 10/30/2006

A BETTER TRUER FRIEND

The mist is winning its way into my reflection and the only thing I see is what I used to be.
Now, I am in this situation that has taken me into a new Universe, the vast sea of a feeling that is free.
How it flows and winds through the stars and I'm taking for granted that everything I see is real.
Sleep whispers in my ear, and I taste a sweetness, so conversant a being is this dream that now I feel.

Nothing is perfect and we know that since time has stopped, but what of the beginning and what of the end?
Jotting down in a hurry, I show myself now that I'm alert and write what I feel, yet how are we to begin?
It's something that stays and never flees if its true, and though we be more of the same, love will always win.
Wishing is where I am and I know not what will happen but stay I will and be I will a better truer friend.

by Cliff Rhodes 09/25/2006

ANOTHER PLACE

*This week, for all you know, I'm the only star that sends my light to you from
so far away in space.*
*I'm here yes, but not so close, that you will know, but here I am, and here I'll
stay.*
*I send my light so you will know that even here; the stars all hear your songs
of laughter and of love*
*You sing so beautiful and so sweet; I cannot overcome the charm of your
melody and the spirit of your fun.*
*How long have you been singing this mood that takes men into such a daze, a
place of so much sweetness and content?*
*You know not, that you have such power and such enchantment to make me
how I am and there is no regret nor repent.*
*This is no infirmity that I have, and it is not a problem from where I am, but
only another place to live and breathe and feel.*
*You must not know that this place exists or you would celebrate the same as I
and rejoice that this is real.*
*Don't worry for my lightness and elevated condition since it has carried me
into another plane of existence.*
*Please carry on as before and just sing, and dance, and say that all is normal
since I would not want so many to insist, that they too could be here too if
only they would continue in persistence.*
*It's not a thing that can be so easily attained since the gift was from you. You
gave me of your sweetness and song and formed its melody into such a spirit
that breathed in me a love that will not die.*
*Soon I'll call you again from this far away star so you'll know that my light
is real and your song is still sweet and pure, but don't think too much or
you'll find out that your spirit too can fly.*

by Cliff Rhodes, 0928/2006

MY SPACE, A PLACE IN SPACE

The computer, so jaded from cataloguing the wasteland of internet names,
finally at day's end can cool off and rest from it's electron chasing games.
Current is off, power is gone, all is quiet, but the game is not lost.
People are resting in quiet repose, but no one is ever alone.
From out of the darkness memory lives and springs like a flower that feeds
on the thrill of sights and sounds and yes, there is love.
But who knows if it's real or commercial or junk?
Wonder and amazement is all around, now wake up!
Everything is passing through time at fast speed.
The planet is spinning around and around, itself, the sun, and the galaxy.
The Earth is moving like a spaceship and moving through time.
Don't wait for too long or the idea will leave.
Spend time with words, and metaphors, and agents, and editors.
Who knows? Maybe you'll make one curious, or cranky, or steamed.
Let's have some fun and bend an old ear, or perk up a younger one
and laugh at our fears. Take on the challenge and you'll be the bettor for it.
Aren't we free to speak, say our peace of mind, and let out that gasp of
expression that's been keeping us dreaming?
Lead on, oh spirit of freedom, and shout our your words.
Let writers jot down in a moment's decision.
For if we wait, time is coming to snatch back the vision,
and leave forever entombed our mind in indecision.

by Cliff Rhodes
08/21/2006

DREAMS OF YOUTH AND AGE

Of all the days when life was young

I'd dream of times when in my teens,

of books being read and sketching was fun,

and Mom and Dad would always come---

to the rescue with money and love,

dollars for the clothes, always clean

and just in the nick of time, my luck

had me scraping a knee so ugly and bloody

but there was my Mom, good so funny

and witty. I'd just have to see

that being so young was sunny

and lovely but nothing forever was free.

I'll pay to the piper that money

I'd borrowed and then I'd scream

Never and never again to be young,

older and older I'll grow, and working is fun.

by Cliff Rhodes
07/01/2006

MY WIFE WANTS A BIRD

Canaries and finches all are flying

around in my mind. One is high

and the other is low, but not in the sky

----both are on a cloud of money and time.

Money I'll have to pay and pay

and still pay—yet time is not free today,

since I'll be the one who'll be saving

the papers and boxes to put in the tray.

The birds are inventing a new style

for me. It's working and paying with my time—

and that's not all. She says I

still need to give feed and water and try

to be good to the birds, since also

there's a cat, and dog or pony of gold,

and more than you could even know.

I'd like another now, maybe a crow!

by Cliff Rhodes
07/10//2006

THE COFFEE BLINK

There she sits in that restaurant,
her hot coffee she sips and she thinks about
who he is, and what does he want?

The waiter pours her another cup and winks.
She thinks, "I hate men who wink."
The waiter thinks, "She must like me, she blinked."

Two thousand miles away he is at home,
hot coffee he sips and thinks alone,
who she is and what does she know?

All the world is moving and turning.
Music plays, and Audrey Hepburn is on T.V., dancing.
She thinks, "How can he be so blasé?
He writes me poems and talks of places
that he doesn't know or can even say the name."

He says to himself that she is most unique and makes his day.
She sings and makes C.D.s and is so famous. He says,
"I wish one day that we could just sit and play the game."

Back in L.A., she takes another sip.
She thinks, "Audrey Hepburn was so hip.
She played chess and was always good at tennis."

Two thousand miles away he takes another drink.
He pours himself a full cup and wants to think.
He says out loud, "I'll bet she is good at tennis
and if we ever play chess, I just let her win,
graciously pour her a cup of coffee, then wink."

by Cliff Rhodes 10/09/2006

WITH LAUGHING AND ROMANCE

Lover, I am so in the other
room that we call another
place that is not of my liking
and we cannot stay fighting.

This place is forever a barrier
to our togetherness that tarries
on and on in my mind forever.
Don't you see you're in my fantasies?

You tell me you can't talk
so I go to the other room.
Now I'm alone and walk and walk
back and forth; soon how soon?

Can't you just give in a little
and compromise some of your demands?
We shouldn't discuss so brittle
our feelings. Nothing is worth this madness.

I wish I had flowers or candy
to give and make it up fast
to you so we could be together at last
again in you room with laughing and romance.

by Cliff Rhodes
January 28, 2007

A VALENTINE FOR YOU

A valentine for all my beautiful female friends on this most special day

Here's to thinking of you and the tracks my soul has made beside you in the way

Even in the night's longest dreams when visions of euphoric fantasy delay

Some artists have their symbolism like trains, but for me valentines return the same

Each year on this day my heart goes to beating like drums, maybe bongos or timpani

For there, in the mirage of beauty and niceties is that sweet feminine company

Maybe your heart would skip just one beat to feel the many of my heart's symphony

Commercial it may be yet returns year after year and pangs and pangs away, ...funny.

If I had a thousand hearts and a thousand wishes I'd divide them all up and give to many

But since I'm just one and there's a million loves I'll just pray for all together

Christ is the one who gave to us all, the love that stays until the end of infinity

His heart I'll share, since this way I'll know that those who love, will be in love forever.

by Cliff Rhodes

02/14/2007

FISHERS OF MEN

They were fishing aimlessly in a fog of self-centeredness

He called them one by one and told them, "Follow me".

He taught them to heal, change hearts, and to give without selfishness.

They awoke him in darkness and cried that they were afraid and could not see.

He calmed the storm and came to them on the waves, touching their hearts.

They were blind and he made them see, and couldn't walk and made them well.

He taught them to repent and to love others and seek the father and live forever.

They couldn't even remain awake in the night to watch for just one hour.

He was taken to be tried and then crucified and on that fateful day of hell.

They saw that rent was the curtain from top to bottom and flung open was the door.

He left heaven's pathway now wide open to those who believe and have reprieve.

Death and sin and hell are conquered and free are all men to follow the son and believe.

Now the fisherman is still with us in spirit and comforts us each and every one.

We read the Bible, we sing, we pray and meditate that some day he'll come.

He'll rule over all the earth and every knee shall bow and yes, his spirit has won.

We now call others to leave their nets, "Follow him".

Leave your boats and rejoice; YOU ARE FREE. Leave your sins willingly and choose which path will it be---Sin, Hate, Destruction, and Death?--or Love, and Liberty and Life. Hallelujah, ---Jesus Christ Arose!

by Cliff Rhodes 04/06/2007

NOT A BLACK AND WHITE PHOTOGRAPH

Passionate I was about the light and dark of shadow
It made me think of things , I don't yet know how,
wavy and translucent in the near dark I say I might could see.
Love and longing could be close to a reality but not even close to real, to me.

I imagine it could have been a dream or wish to see more of magic,
not that it would appear to be a fantasy but not either or both yet not tragic.
I looked deeper within the play of light and shadow and there she lingered,
as if in repose, frozen at a moment in her thoughts; then I saw just her hand
and fingers.

Resting there as if to beckon the observer into the beautiful space between
sleep and dreams,
She summoned and called and appeared as if guiding the ship onto smooth
waves of steam.
Not yet hot upon the ocean it rolled on and on upon the soft grassy plane of
water and sea.
My ship was sailing but I knew not where but on and on I went like a
machine, smooth and free.

The photograph was not a painting but not a vision and not a wish for any
gold or silver,
still it was another sign that all the world, in patient loving tender instruction
was still a welcome lover.
Lonely at times and always a loving mother, the Earth, she called to another
friend who only said hello,
nonchalantly, and ever with great respect of such a passionate pose, looking
and admiring , she so mellow.

I saw her then and still see her now in my mind's eye when such similar light
and shadow caresses my ship
as I sail on and on across the dark expanse of time and distance and space
within this life long trip.
I wait for my dreams in the night to take form and lift me up into that realm
where eyes no longer see,
where ears no longer hear, and tongue can no longer taste any rare sweet
thing, but memory.

The star blazes on and I'm guided now, not by my sight but by my longing for knowledge
of rare and wondrous beauty to behold as my journey is beginning to be more poetic and I pledge,
to always stop along the way and taste that rare moment of truth when I realize my weakness
is not my calamity but my friend and so sincere and elegantly beautiful still is love, the true witness.

by Cliff Rhodes
06/14/2007

THE BREATH OF HAPPINESS

My breath caught quick as a new surprise and I did feel your presence
as if I imagined that you were here or in a dream such as an essence.
I looked and there among the stars was such a bright light that I paused
and stared as if a glance would not be enough to catch me from my fall.

Into love and happiness I fell and never feared for one moment in time. Not
that I could fall so far that your love would not lift my spirit to fly.
The wind, now a slight breeze, stirred strands of long hair and slight fabric
to wave and linger while dancing on magic and air and was so fantastic.

I witness today that a breath is not just a life, and not just an awakening.
So it is true and good and giving of love and giving of spirit, a winning.
Both of us have won and we now have a treasure that never will die.
We have a memory that will live on forever and balanced eternal on high.

You see what I see so clearly, is that Spirit that walks through our minds.
We share together our thoughts, our feelings, our days and our nights.
Have you been to see for yourself that the waves of the ocean are real?
Try now and test if you can see that salt spray upon sandy shore to feel.

Now that these lines have been read and you've seen this forever spirit.
There's only one thing left to do and you know you'll never want to quit.
Give your heart to your true love and take away that pain and disdain.
Find your Spirit and dare to share just one moment in loving refrain.

by Cliff Rhodes
06/20/2007

THE NEW BLUE MOON

Hope springs new eternal and upon this one thing I challenge YOU
my friend, my love, my essence of such beauty and charm; it's true.
There is always that bright light on yonder hill so lit in moonlight blue
that seems like such a mountain to climb and always ahead of us looms.

We gaze at visions beyond our site that only we can see in hazy shades
of green and grey that drift upon our imagination, yet still never fades.
Our gaze is true and we know that wild beyond even our rarest dreams
lies that distant shore where happy times will once again return to please.

Lord, guide her through her trials and toils to rise upon those lofty wings
of eagles and angels and flying clouds that lift her past the pain that stings.
Like fiery darts and arrows bright of hurt they keep her asking too long
for relief, but send her peace and soon she'll sing other new love songs.

It's only time that's left and slowly brings that quiet place for rest and sleep
when dreams so real and light makes bright the path, makes sure our feet.
Sleep on oh angel of sound, oh lightness of voice, oh treasure of beauty.
We'll meet in music when you awake and turn our ears so breath may soothe.

Beauty is within and without and calls me to hear so pure that voice,
but eye beholds and sees her face, so attractive it is that there's no choice.
I'll never take away my eyes or ears unless my heart, it's beating dies.
For she alone can make that rhythm rhyme with heart and ears and eyes.

I'll play forever that memory again I've grown so fond to rewind,
turning over and over inside those songs of love and life and time.
Peace to you, my friend, again and thanks forever and maybe soon
you'll dance and laugh with light and joy to see that moon so blue, so true.

Get well soon.

by Cliff Rhodes
06/23/2007

LOVE LIKE ORION

I walk and love follows me. I run and love finds me and overtakes me.

I cannot escape from love because all of my days and nights are for thee.

Love has found me and will not release me and I am happy and pleased.

Wisdom also is a part of love, is together with love, and wisdom too is free.

Give respect and honor to love and she will give you wisdom, all you need.

Keep wisdom always in thy mind to guard thy path and she will run with speed.

Love is life and life is love and never is one without the other, so we can breathe.

Love is strong as death, and jealousy as cruel as the grave but wisdom is reprieve.

Take me now and hold me close and set my spirit free, free to fly and be with thee.

I charge thee now to see me real, as real as real can be, not dreams or visions

nor fantasies you see, and my heart is touched always if only by your whispers.

When you sing my dreams come alive and whispers become reality intense.

Now I sleep, my head on a pillow, clothed in dreams of love and wisdom and truth.

No moonlight can soothe so well as the sound that drifts from her lips so sweet, so cool.

I hear the sound and I cannot find who she is or where she flies. Oh it's you.

Only now is that new vision of laughter and dancing and we go on and on.

Bright Jupiter is rising, alas in the distance and its light touches you like Orion.

In space I drift on in my dreams as my soul sees the stars, and what is on the horizon.

Today I ran ten miles and ten times love almost caught me but then she let me win.

She knows all along that I run but cannot escape since it's my heart, she's always in.

I walk and love follows me. I run and love finds me and wins again, and again.

by Cliff Rhodes – 07/04/2007

THE ECHO DOES NOT RETURN

The echo I wait for does not come back to me.
I shout and sing but the melody returns free.
There is nothing in this void of space but sea.

The waves break over this rocky shore.
Salt spray I feel but no sound forms.
No words are there upon my mind torn.

I am broken and in despair as I feel this loneliness.
She knows this place since she gave me it's address.
I return here from time to time for the test.

I am here to make peace with love,
to take what love gives from above,
because my heart is empty and undone.

I don't care that I ache since my burden is lifted.
I gave from my heart together with my mind, the gift.
Nothing I'll ask in return because it was from spirit.

I am an empty vessel now ready to be filled.
This ocean is so vast, so real, such a vision.
No end in sight is thy love, so much joy to give.
I am ready now again to love and to live in spirit.
Oh God, use me again if it be thy will.

by Cliff Rhodes
07/09/2007

THE MUSE MAKES ME BLUE

Blue now, I'm always blue, for you
I was never meant to be so blue.
That, I thought, was for someone else.
Now, shadows pass across myself.

No beauty should move so soon
from here to there, now nowhere.
We talked of almost nothing new.
You went and left my life, everywhere.

You leave no news, no clues
of your life, your love, your laughter.
Your words disappeared, so blue.
What happens now hereafter?

I am forgotten among so many.
The others are beyond my comprehension.
They are so excellent and friendly.
I can't match their attention.

Say hello in a dream or a thought.
I'll be there for a time until lost.
Soon I'll fade to gray.
Soon I'll be gone away.

You'll forget my words, my face.
I'll never be so bright as this day.
My color now is always blue.
One day, soon I'll see another muse.

But to me she'll always look, like you.
Clouds cover my rainbow, all my hues.
There is no sunshine to break through.
Blue now, always blue, for you;
I was never meant to be so blue.

Break the impasse and say my name.
Say hello to play the game.
Only you can take away my pain.

Gone away, this chance we waste.
Love was never meant to stay.

Now I dream forever. Dreams are made for heaven.
The Muse makes me blue, I'll always think of you.

by Cliff Rhodes
07/21/2007

A SPATIAL PLANE OF HAPPINESS

No place on Earth, to change the day,
no space to say what's on my brain.
So, a little detour is in order to get away.
Machines are moving and wheels turning all the way.

Inside of emotions not needed until now,
wrapped in a nice cocoon so no one finds how,
is this passage clearly marked, yet never found,
by those who like to stay in sadness with frowns.

I open the door and there stands happiness ready to go.
Take me to that place where no longer is blue, nor misplaced hope, nor ill
will, nor suspicion, nor fear but good times all aglow.
I'm ready and willing to follow my spirit to guide even in snow.

Cold wind sounds the alarm and seems frozen, ready to accuse.
I run to that plane, that spatial, that allusion, where nothing confuses.
My life begins again and no turmoil enters in. No, time is not computed,
just entombed in it's own delusion , that ruse I've found is yet still true.

I can because I will and I will because I can and so unfurls that banner.
I see that flag always flies high even in cold winds and is never tattered.
It sails on the breeze of hope and truth and follows none before it.
Never has reference nor need of anger, this allusion, and always it wins.

Love and happiness still win despite howls of laughter from sadness,
and gloom is still doomed to glide the mists of distress and crashes in sand.
My blue is now gone the same way of the past as snow that never lasts.
It has melted with sunlight and rays from above in God's fiery blast.

Love always brings hope to overcome confusion and tears down walls.
Delusion is so forlorn and not much worth the effort, not even to talk.
Why discuss mistakes and get frozen in space when there is nothing at all.
What existed may be lost or wasn't even a thought, so how could I fall?

I may not have fallen, I may not be distraught, just thinking of this song.
The muse gave me a rhyme for a reason and a time for the season so long.
She says that all is fallen that never falls,
and all is sad that was never in sadness.

To never love, never has love, and to never let go, never goes.
I go on to yet another, that other place, that other space, like a ghost.
I know where I go and I know why I went but do you know where you go?
I shine in darkness and give light in obscurity. What do you give to know?

Give of yourself freely expecting nothing in return.

by Cliff Rhodes
07/21/2007

LOVE IS AN INFINITE SEASON

Why not change from love to some other emotion?
Time is different and one is not of the same volition.
It makes no difference whether or not the one loved gives back.
The emotion is still there in the heart and the mind and is fantastic.

She does not have to respond or emote any word or whisper.
The rhythm of her heartbeat is felt within my spirit.
It lingers long after her words have disappeared into the air so thin.
Her hint of care and the caress of her being is still present.

How can I know this or even presume to believe that it exists?
How does it feel; that emotion that knows and whispers only of visits?
Does her spirit say, "Hello"? Does she venture to commune?
Who knows what love knows and who dares to question a muse?

There is no muse, only some frolic of word play that tends to amuse.
"She" might get some laughter from that word and request a tune.
Though I would be lacking in song or note, I would defer and ask of her.
"Please sing me to sleep tonight and hum sweet melodies in my ear."

I never tire of love or of song or of melody made in perfect pitch.
In all the world there never was so beautiful a voice so rich.
She MUST be an angel or a vision or even some reborn Greek muse.
Since Love is an infinite season and constantly seeks to renew.

She springs forth eternal without comment or word or response.
I'm waiting for the snow to melt or the river to flow or the clouds to pass.
She never needs to be verified or quantified or explained, even an ounce.
Love is an infinite season and returns in time as time returns at last.

Now she speaks and everyone waits, even to hear her whisper.
She opens her mouth and the spirit comes forth so tender and sweet.
The flower revives on the shelf, not watered for days, was dead, now alive.
The smell of jasmine fills the air because she thought only in her mind.

Her glad heart beats gently in time with mine and her breath I breathe.
Now I can live again because she passed my way and made me glad.
Though the words make no sense to the commoner among us we see.
   by Cliff Rhodes 07/24/07

LOVE IS STILL AFTER YOU
HAPPINESS IS ALL AROUND YOU

Love never breaks
it's only a heart ache.
You can't fight love,
'cause it's all from above.
I love you too.
You know it's true.

You'll never get away,
'cause after I'm gone away
Love is still after you,
Happiness is all around you.

I never said I'd stay
until that glorious day,
when you wake up and see
it's not entirely me.

It's not my fault.
It was easy to talk,
of love and laughter
and all the lessons that you taught.

I learned to love even though
you never gave me back, oh no,
the same I gave to you, so soon.
I could never get to you, so cool.

Love is still after you
and it will get you too, anyway.

You sing that song
like it doesn't ever belong.
You always prefer to sing of love lost.

You belong to love
and you can't get away,
not so soon, not this day.
You can't hide it all that way.

You can't say it's not real
'cause your heart will still reveal,
that love is all around you, see.
Even though you think, you are free;
you'll always belong to love.,
'cause love lets you breathe,
and feel, and see,
all the stars above.

Love is still after you.
Happiness is all around you.

After I'm gone, someday, it won't be long.
Love is still here, will always be here,
even when you sing this song.

Love will never let you get away.
Maybe though, it's not me you see in your moon.
God is in love with you.
His love will save you, anyway.

Love has found you.
Happiness is inside you.

Peace

by Cliff Rhodes
07/30/2007

LOVE IS A HEALING EMOTION

Love is a healing emotion that takes us into another dimension,
makes us tireless dreamers, takes us into a new religion.
We never knew we could transfer that feeling into a sense of freedom.
We become free from our center of self, our one-sided sea of blah.

How interesting to be concerned for another's welfare, her health,
her presence of being, her friendship, her sense of calm, her breath.
Does she feel afraid? Does she seem tense? Does she not want to talk?
Why all this worry, all this bother, this madness, this desperation of loss?

Because, she is there among the myriad of stars that have light and being.
She alone is calmness that beckons some part of soul to begin revealing.
After the inspiration a second skin is exposed so that it might be hurt,
to let her break the heart and hurt that part that wishes for only a word.

There is no why or where or when some love may return but only peace.
Harmony and beauty have somehow aligned their rhythm to stay free.
Lively euphoria takes over and now there is no such thing as entropy.
In love there exists no still water because the spirit is healthy.

God has blessed us with love so we may be thrilled to know new life.
Love is newness of life, open to wonder and amazement, smiling inside.
Happiness is her pretty spirit that has created a new place to meet.
Our spirits can fly and reach beyond those who cannot dream.

Our eyes now see because no physical boundary exists to restrain.
Nothing can keep my spirit from flying off in any direction or plane.
I take flight and cross the world and fly above all that is Earthly and safe.
Yet, when I approach I dare not speak because she has not made a way.

Coming back is lonely but reassuring that on some other spatial plane,
there exists that pathway to love, to happiness, to her playful space.
The place where she is happier and in better spirits makes me feel fine.
I cherish the thought that she is happy and safe, even if with another mind.

My mind is her playground and all my thoughts have turned into jasmine.
Her perfume is my feelings, my concern, and my best wishes, all the time.
Love is a healing emotion that never feels discontent nor unrest.
I could wait for an eternity and feel the same emotion, take the same test.

Waiting is such joy and such anticipation that never ends nor tires.
There is no despair, no depression nor resentment since love inspires.
Love is a healing emotion that has taken me into another dimension.
I am now free from myself, from my own concern, from my own vision.

by Cliff Rhodes
08/02/2007

AMAZING LOVE

Rising above the boundless horizon that not one person can challenge
is that unfettered love that never ceases, never slows, and never dies.
Beauty and strength and all the moody emotions never see that visage.
There is no comprehension of love living eternally in wisdom's eyes.

To see false egos and realize misguided opportunistic struggles
plays entertaining games within myriad minds of famous past lovers.
They find their own fates among rusted, worn out old car jungles
of discarded heaps, never recovering from first rejection love discovers.

To rise with the morning sun and stretch and yawn and praise God
seems like some unknown emotion to doleful depressed past lovers.
How can just a weak man, unknown to modern love be such a shock
to the famous players of great love and go about life without any cares?

Should not he be in sadness at rejection since love is not synchronized?
He loves greatly but never is returned any one word of recognition.
Those he loves can give nothing in form of friendship, even sanitized.
Those of the sea of sadness make no sense of this light and airy vision.

To wait forever for some other love to be brought into the amazing light
seems like a boring decision on the part of someone who thinks he loves.
He says that he will wait for something to occur. Could that be right?
What could be happening, in body, in spirit, in heart, in mind, to us?

God's amazing love transforms all of us into new creatures who care not
for the object of this world's love and its troubles that separate friends.
The spirit is not torn into pieces when one loves and the other will stop.
One person loves and another does not, so which one in the end wins?

Love is amazing and builds towers beyond the reach of those who do not
continue in love and they cease to be of importance, even to themselves.
Life goes on for those without love, for those who pretend love will stop.
To join that sad parade is beyond comprehension and not one for myself.

Love is a mystical realm that cares not for those who are lost in confusion.

For those who dare not love and who cannot love, it has no sympathy.
To those who can only love once, it smiles with amusement and attrition.
For she who laughs at love, wisdom finds her and promptly gives empathy.

My heart races to find wings and lifts up on currents of promise and hope.
All the world is not sad and all the world is not forlorn and full of despair.
She of beauty and grace will continue to find place among stars of gold.
Love is eternal, love is all around us, love is everywhere, even in the air.

by Cliff Rhodes
08/05/2007

BOTH BROKENHEARTED

Brokenhearted, both of us lingered
in between two moments in time.
Two spirits pause, sharing something treasured,
both hearts aching to know why.

The other, she and I, never made it easy
to claim victory over each other.
We slowly separated because of vanity.
Now comes the hurt and the wonder.

How can my heart be in such sorrow?
Life is amazing to have so much love.
I am in sadness and in love, but how?
One is blending slowly into the other.

Heart ache is now heart joy as some
wonderful wild spirit becomes a beckoning angel.
Dance the dance of life, she talks of love.
It can be so temporary, and so temperamental.

Dream of love now, before it's over.
We shouldn't separate, since our hearts are both tender.
Your love did not know that you were her friend.
So, at least you are mine now, if only for this night.
We should just dance and we will win.

Brokenhearted, both of us lingered
in between two moments in time.

by Cliff Rhodes
08/07/2007

LOVE NEVER DIES

Sunlight begins glittering off the horizon and makes starting leaps
into windows not completely closed from the night's sleep.
Eyes open and begin another amazing day of being blessed by God.
Courage lights up in hearts all over the world, starting to imagine what?

Does she think about me? Has she another? Will she remember me?
Why, oh why, am I still in love and why is my heart full of laughter?
Her long dark hair is in my mind and she constantly finds my dreams.
Her soft beautiful voice is still taking me into the ozone, now only higher.

Another is taking my memory from a long time ago and I remember
that it was a similar dream of being taken half-way to heaven only
to fall upon the rocks of reality, hurting my poor spirit with only a word,
then having to go on again into the darkness, alone without light, free.

Why do we not want to be free, yet we crave freedom, but our spirit flies.
Yet spirits cannot fly without love, but love will not let you free, why?
Ask God why we should be in love and stay in love and love never dies.
No person knows the answer or we would all know why we cry.

Young and old, strong and weak are slaves to love and love's ways.
To live and to die and to love are all human things we cannot escape.
To seek life's best and hold onto love until death is defeated is to play.
Such a beautiful game it is with life and love that death is only a shame.

Sunlight beckons those thirsty souls who never drink from life's cup.
Open your soul and let love pour in from above and fill up your life.
You never breathe if breath is not taken and water is for your dry tongue.
How can eyes see in darkness if there is not light to give some pain to eye.

A painful heart is only an ache and love never breaks what is flooding.
Emotions flood the soul and prick the heart to find resolutions in time.
Never is one mended better before the heart ache since love isn't winning.
After love has won then the mend makes better the person to fly so high.

She can spread her wings and fly above all cares and sorrows forever.
Never has love made some obstruction a thought to make time undone.
Love never considers distance a great problem or even being together.
Mystery of mysteries transpires and transforms and dreams are now one.

To never say goodbye, to never talk of sorrow, to never walk away
is so much more than minds need to think about when love is here now.
Breathe love and think love and to speak of love is all we need for to stay.
We should keep love in some place where it would never see any frown.

Have fun in love, and make laughter even in the rain, and I will run to you.
Call me when you need one who wants only your peace and happiness.
See me in your mind when you need a friend who wants only to be true.
Words on paper are never even close to real feelings that minds express.

The real reason the two of us don't talk is because words are lost.
There is no word to express our feelings except in some love song.
You have only to sing and I'll listen while waves of emotion tell the cost.
You sing of love and I listen to love and soon love takes me along.

by Cliff Rhodes
08/13/2007

LOVE IS ALWAYS NEW

Love is never an old love, is always a new love since it never goes away.
Age upon age and love comes back still new as if those who have loved
never left her brilliant side only for one moment while she, loyal stayed.
We brighten and then dim but love has a fire that never fades from above.

Cherish the thoughts of love while you may, for upon some musical note
of more somber tone, that chance is turned into mist and soon is ghostly
gray as if it never had flesh and blood but was just a wisp of smoke.
Carry your memory closely within your heart before words fade slowly.

Imagine that love is real before reality steals it away and makes it folly.
Love is only a joke when you let it go and then it is as a dream you need.
Need becomes a vision and then only God can give any breath to breathe.
Friend upon friend passes and never one gives any hint of feelings real.

Guard not your emotions for fear of exposing your need for love.
All of us need love, who breathe, who speak, who laugh, and who cry.
Words are not a solution but somehow find form to express joy and fun.
Love is fun, is laughter, is pain, is sorrow, is needing that other light.

Take your chance and love while you can before love is recalled to others.
There are those who need love more than you and love will pass you by.
Heed love's call and rejoice that God has chosen you to inspire another.
Talk to the one who loves you and take all of Earth's passing to fly.

Love will take you flying above all envy and all turmoil and all pain,
never letting you fall or stumble or seem ordinary or plain nor demanding.
Give yourself to love that will never fade into days of regret or disdain.
The solution is simple, only to open your heart and let love find it's wings.

Play in the ocean, gliding upon wings of water and break to the surface.
Soar upon the pillows of clouds breathing in fresh air that fills your lungs.
Quit your old days of hiding in darkness where not one word gives chase.
Games with words and sounds and thoughts and meanings are such fun.

Why shy away from only conversation when nothing can hurt to try?
In love there is no fear, no condemnation, no tragedy, only true peace.
To break open that spirit, that underneath skin and feel real light
brings such joy and health to your being as if to emerge into a new eye.

Love is not a banana peel that slips under bare feet
but neither is it skid free. You just have to read yourself into the dream.

by Cliff Rhodes
08/14/2007

LOVE IS A LIVING SPIRIT

Love is a living spirit that finds you even when you are invisible.
Hide your soul in the deepest corner of Earth and love will seek you out.
Never can you withdraw into that darkness so you become unreachable.
Though you try not to talk the spirit sends words that are found.

Your loneliness is tragic and beyond comprehension, but I understand.
Never have you so wanted to communicate even to some poor stranger.
To give voice to your anguish, your turmoil, your pure agony so sad,
until this day and this time has finally now arrived and beckons to hear.

Let your fears be put away and allow your heart to reveal true revelation.
There is no reason to find fault with anyone other than your own love.
Let your love now be revealed into pure ecstasy and abandon, a transition.
Change into a spiritual being, a light bearer, who brings gifts from above.

If you hide your love and friendship then you only hurt your own being.
How can love heal and change hearts and bring a new spirit into your life?
By living in the spirit and breathing in the gift from God and being free.
Let go of those ways of self destruction and corruption that bring strife.

Love is a living spirit that is constantly changing all those around.
If you are not changing or being changed for the better then you are sad.
Truly the greatest burden is to change one who doesn't want to be found.
If you hide your love, or hide your spirit, then you never have a chance.

Take the chance and the opportunity to give spiritual comfort to only one.
If you find just one then you have found yourself and realize the need.
We all need to help some friend and bring them without being judged.
Help them into the light and give them comfort and friendship to see.

God will open their eyes and open their ears so that they become free.
Let them be free from their own turmoil, free from their own chains.
They soon will be able to live in the spirit as all loving beings who believe.
Christ's love is the answer and never your own and forever will it remain.

by Cliff Rhodes
08/17/2007

LOVE LINGERS ON AND ON

Love doesn't run away and play as if it doesn't exist,
so why presume that it will disappear if you don't say hi.
The song you sing doesn't bring us closer together in this mist.
A ghostly shape is now what our friendship used to be, but why?

Fear is what I think controls the day and dim facts of uncertainty.
Real love has never been that controlling but will never fade away.
No love who claims so bright a star has chosen a path of discontinuity.
How could love be, if love was so real that it wouldn't stay and stay?

When you think of me next I will be as I was when we first were friends,
the same as it was when you first read my words, and knew in your heart
that the words you read were from a friend and that friend was in spirit
above all the very closest of friends whose heart was near and not far.

My heart is with your heart and will always be a friend of love, your love.
Love never fails to linger on and on and stay near not far, not so strange.
Friends should continue to communicate, to talk, and not be shunned.
Is love so dangerous to you that you have the necessity to hide it away?

Love is not your enemy and is always wishing you the best of the best.
Waiting patiently is love, knowing one day that you will be love's friend.
I have chosen this way so you can give me that most difficult of tests.
I will be as if I was not, hiding my love inside, living as if I never did exist.

My love is always reserved for you, is always near that heart of hearts.
Love is happiness and a warm inspiring feeling that passes through me.
Spirit hears my love that I have for you and is sending light into dark.
My love arrives to you still, through my prayers, even if we don't speak.

Love lingers on and on, into the day, into the night, and into your heart.
Sing me to sleep; I hear you now, even in my dreams, even in your absence.
Love lingers on and on, into my dreams; forever you'll be my bright star.
Mist upon mist and dreams go by, yet love will be real, if only an essence.

by Cliff Rhodes
08/20/2007

LOVE SLEEPS INSIDE TWO MIRRORS MADE OF GOLD

Love sleeps inside two mirrors made of gold.
One reflects the heart, the other the soul.
When love awakes she looks and sees the ocean.
Heart says to love, "Not yet love, tide is still too low.

Sleep on, oh love, there is naught reason for to wake.
The tide is still too low and the waves will not take us away.
We should not awake for there are yet no waves ."
Love sleeps on and dreams of laughter and of play.

The sun is bright and now arises for the glory of some new day star.
Love still sleeps on, inside two mirrors, for there are yet no waves.
She dreams of songs to sing, of chords to play on her golden guitar.
Love sleeps and dreams of waves, yet still and calm that ocean stays.

Love laughs and plays inside her dreams of sun and salt and spray.
She sees upon the horizon now, so vague that crest that makes her day.
One wave appears so giant now so bold and out she goes to play.
Underneath her feet she feels that link between soul and ocean slide away.

No heart could tell this love that inside two mirrors sleeps she still.
One reflects the heart of some poor lover the other his soul made of gold.
Whose heart is this that would not tell love she sleeps against her will?
My heart 'tis not for waves are crashing there within so noisy and so bold.

Love is in my heart and dreams awake and we upon the ocean together go.
Wild upon the tops of waves and slides our souls on rivers of glass.
We fly upon the wind and waves and laugh in bright sun, words unspoken.
Love sleeps inside two mirrors made of gold and never stops to laugh.

by Cliff Rhodes
08/21/2007

EMOTIONAL MYSTERY

Beautiful vibrantly colored flowers crowd the illusion
of feelings that plant themselves inside the psyche.
Calm and soothing melodies find almost heart-felt decisions.
Smooth and cool waters flow within her dry eyes.

Since doors don't open and words won't flow smoothly
there reveals itself the presence of a bridge over troubled waters.
This bridge goes nowhere and is only a temporary finality
of indecision that predominates problem solving and falters.

Failure to follow through to any extent gives evidence
of some confusion and mystery of past difficult relations.
Sadness is not exactly evident nor is it used as a short residence
for keeping attention on yourself and away from trying situations.

This scenario has so many troubles and so much heart-breaking emotion
that will not come out and surface to become a part of the past.
Once feelings take over and the truth becomes your ultimate decision
then the past is finally made just a short memory and not a heavy cast.

Unaffectionate friends who don't get involved become brilliant flowers
that can be used as decorations that hide the real trouble, deep love.
It is so real that it must be hidden away and covered up to gain power.
To love is to lose power and become weaker and affectionate, so run.

by Cliff Rhodes
08/22/2007

LOVE STORY OF THE HIGHLAND PRINCESS

Long, long ago and far, far away lived this most beautiful princess.
Not one fair maiden in any village could touch the purity of her heart
and not one person ever had such a beautiful voice as she possessed.
All day long and into the evening she would practice even into the dark.

Along with her singing she was also the most brilliant student of archery.
She would arise early in the morning to practice shooting at targets.
Never once did she even come close to missing the small apples, so juicy.
Each one was placed exactly and precisely balanced atop fence pickets.

The range was exceeding and always she would wait until exactly sunrise.
Then after singing a long note, high G flat, she would let her arrows fly.
With the sun in her eyes to practice her concentration and her note, high
G flat, she would make her arrows, one by one, pierce each target's eye.

Her fame grew and spread near and far all across the Highland country.
Young men became so enamored with her singing, so beautiful, but also
with her archery skills and would stand and watch before sunrise to see.
One handsome man, his heart beating wildly inside his chest, waited alone.

He climbed a large apple tree that was only one of many along the picket.
Perched high in the limbs of the seemingly sturdy apple tree he stayed.
Crowds began to gather even before daybreak and then the princess
made her ritual march out to the pickets to balance the apples to remain.

They stayed just as she put them one by one atop the picket except one.
It began to wobble and move maybe because of the breeze or some spirit.
Almost imperceptible it appeared to move to the handsome man above.
He was in just the right position to reach down and align the apple to fit.

Fit it he did so that exactly atop the picket it would stay for the princess.
Though in his reach, he overextended the load for the limb and his hold.
Crack went the limb, breaking! Blazing came the sun, shining!... a mess!
The most beautiful thing about the whole convoluted ordeal was the note.

The beautiful princess let that high G flat fill all the hills and valleys.
For some mysterious moment it lingered in the ears of the poor man.
He heard as if it was an angel singing one beautiful and glorious melody.
The pain was almost nonexistent as the princess's arrow went, thwack!

As the handsome man's poor body hit the pickets all the apples fell at once.
For only one moment the princess was completely stunned and amazed.
How had all of the apples fallen at once? Then she saw him at the fence.
He was not moving, not even breathing, and all the people gasped, crazed.

The princess ran as fast as she could and fell upon the man so distressed.
He didn't breathe so she breathed for him, placing her lips upon his.
Moment by moment she feared the worst and then he slowly took a breath.
The family surgeon came and brought the pliers to extract the arrow tip.

It was firmly lodged in his chain mail. She had really knocked him out.
All the Highland villagers celebrated that glorious day since all was well.
The cupid princess had found her mark. It was all around the town.
The note, high G flat, had found his heart even though he wasn't dead.

He told all the villagers that the princess's lips tasted like honey dew.
Her breath was as sweet as jasmine and her long dark hair was soothing
as a spring breeze as it touched his cheeks, and her eyes were like moons.
In his mind were stars in heaven as her hands caressed like angels' wings.

The princess continued singing notes in high G flat and was still excellent
with the bow and arrow as well as having great accuracy in bright light.
Beautiful music would fill the highland hills even early at the picket fence.
The handsome man would now line her apples up for her one by one to fit.

Each picket had an apple exactly fitted to the top of the point, balanced.
Every arrow let fly would have a note sung before its release, high G flat.
Every morning would have a sunrise and every apple would be lanced.
Each arrow let fly would also bring a kiss to the young handsome man.

Cupid's arrow had found it's mark, although mistakenly, and he has best
lived to tell this tale among all highland villagers and among all people.
The moral of the story goes like this. If a beautiful princess is having target
practice and singing in G flat, be sure you have your chain mail on, please.

by Cliff Rhodes
08/23/2007

TWO RIDERS APPROACHING

The beautiful green forest is speckled with light patches filtering in from above. Two riders meet by chance going in two different directions and for a few moments in time the two ride together, side by side, without words. Only slight glances and an occasional nod are all that is needed. For a short time they ride together until the road separates into two different lanes. One goes to the left and the other leads on to the right.

Beautiful day has sprung up and sends rays of light across green trees.
Light plays games in the deep forest and in the distance I see a rider.
The shape is different somehow and I see it takes the form of beauty.
She approaches now and I find upon close examination a light in her eyes.

No words find their voice and this rider I know from some other time.
She takes the reigns of her horse and slowly guides her to almost stop.
We hesitate for some moments in time and gaze into each others' eyes.
The horses snort and pull their necks up and down, impatient to trot.

We hold them together there and make them wait and wait to get our fill.
I never did get enough time to look into that face so beautifully nice.
The shape of her eyes, her long hair, and her smile creates a memory still.
Her long dress spills over the sides of the horse and her shape is divine.

Her eyes take one last look into mine. I freeze, then she kicks her horse.
We both separate and I wheel my horse around in the middle of the road.
I catch up to her and we brush against each other for one moment more.
The road ahead separates and soon I'll turn back to my own way chosen.

Moments upon moments are frozen in time to be remembered forever.
I'll never escape this memory of our last meeting in this land of love.
Memory given in friendship and love can never be taken away, not ever.
Two doves take flight in the trees ahead and wing on into the sky above.

Light speckles the pathway and a cool breeze plays across my face.
I look again at her and our eyes meet for the last time, then look away.
Two paths lead away, one to the left and the other on ahead to the right.
Dark trees block the light as I wheel my horse to the right and sigh, again.

by Cliff Rhodes
08/25/2007

BLUE DIAMONDS INTO THE DARK SKY

Blue turquoise laced with velvet red, the sky was vibrant in shades of blue.
Black clouds came racing out of nowhere to invade the beautiful sunset.
Fast moving, billowing and ominous, they instantly created a new mood.
Where once there were blue diamonds, now boiling, was dark rainy regret.

Her words don't exist and memory is mixed up to the point of confusion.
Harmony and happiness make music temporarily and there is still blue sky.
Blue breaks through and patches of light flicker with the sun's infusion.
I am in a state of transition, fading from blue and back again into time.

My mind takes me back to a time of love regained, an apparent illusion.
Love itself is an illusion of sunlight and blue sky that hides dark clouds.
Perfection that never has an undercurrent is just a thin decoration
So beautiful is the surface and once the top is revealed, truth is found.

Beautiful truth is to be accepted and cherished fervently even in love.
Love adores her devotees but sometimes covers up awaiting dark clouds.
When truth and love walk hand in hand then blue sky reigns all above us.
Pray love, won't you wait a little longer and remain while I am astounded?

Years have passed by and time has recorded many loves and lovers.
Through time, ideas and memories have stuck to the rocks which survive.
Etched into their marble and granite surfaces are recorded lovers' words.
Remember me, oh love, for my suffering and my ecstasy, great divine.

Blue diamonds of love's words and love's emotion play again through time.
I gather into my hand those royal blue gems that have floated out of ether.
Grasping them I toss them up into the air, now boiling with trouble inside.
Underneath that surface of emotion and exuberance lies doubt and fear.

Blue diamonds of love's favorite words are tossed about to and fro.
They mix and meander and find some resolute person who likes to listen.
Hear now love's words whose meanings have been passed along like gold.
Words are golden having left the lover. They soon becomes blue diamonds.

Echoing and sounding round and round, they are transformed into more.
Becoming feelings and emotions, they ring into the heart of one who hears.
Now you are not alone since you have heard these sounds take form.
Completing the circle love has returned from my heart to your heart.

Cherish my thoughts that are recorded here and if it so please your mood.
Throw back into the ocean of loneliness only some words, one or two.
So that I may also find within my awaiting mind some emotion some clue.
Sing of love and truth that I too may catch blue diamonds from you.

by Cliff Rhodes
08/27/2007

A BEDTIME STORY FOR DREAMERS

My eyes are getting heavy and it is almost dreaming time. I relax and lie down because there is no reason to resist that heaviness that has been claiming my time and my attention. I finally close my eyes, a welcome relief after such a long day. Time dilates and I am transported into another dimension where sight and sound are no longer relative to my previous world. Love asks if I am ready to continue along the journey and I answer that everything is fine.

I notice that love is so radiant and so beautiful and she is anxious to continue our journey so I say, "Yes, I am ready, love." A slight breeze of cool fragrant air enters my awareness and I am so comfortable, even though I feel so anxious for the beginning of my journey and I feel my heart is making a steady pounding as anticipation dominates all of my mind and the journey begins to unfold and take precedence. All of my previous dreams have begun this way and then elevated to extreme and rare circumstances where all of my imagination could not even begin to invent or think up situations that would reach to anything near this level of fantasy. We catch each other's hand and just a mere touch opens up a surge of awareness that claims victory over the present and we are transported, not into the past or even the future, but another location in the "near" present. A door opens and we enter, wherever this place is, and instantly we notice that there is music and laughter and people are all around us, Although they are not any people we know, they are very friendly and we talk about nothing important and we begin to discus the things that are insignificant and of almost totally no consequence and then love motions me to follow her and quickly I enter another room with her, a very large but empty room. I look around and notice that there are no flowers in the room and I quickly call out to the air that it would be nice to have some fresh red roses to make the room look a little nicer. So, instantly in a clear crystal green vase, a dozen red roses appear exactly in the center of a small round table placed in front of a tall ornate mirror. Love says that it is not necessary and they disappear immediately. I look at love and she looks at me and then we both look into the mirror. Lights and wavy lines of distortion obscure our view of ourselves and then as if we have found a clear channel on the radio, we are standing there in front of the mirror staring at ourselves. I have on my tuxedo and love is so beautiful, dressed in an elegant evening gown. We then decide to go back to the crowded room and dance for hours and hours stopping only to sip champagne all through the night. I love to look into love's eyes when she is dancing and the smell of her perfume is so extravagant that sometimes I feel faint just to be close to her when we are dancing. Suddenly an alarm sounds and the band picks up their instruments and they quickly disappear through a curtain backstage. I look all around and everyone is hurrying and leaving through several different doors all around the room. One bright lady looks at love and says that it is getting light and it's almost time to wake up.

Love grabs my hand and as we enter the foyer two doors appear. She leans close to my ear before she lets go of my hand to disappear and whispers, "Tomorrow night, ...same time, same place."

by Cliff Rhodes--08/31/2007

LOVE SEARCHES FOR SPIRIT

Love needs spirit to carry its mood into the heart,
wants a willing hand to guide and assure truth,
that through thick and thin there remains that star.
Let us go back farther into time when love was new.

You never were aware that love could fade away.
The first thing that came into your mind was that love
was from heaven and would never leave, never betray.
You were right. Love never left, but love is from above.

Love doesn't stay when there is a heart, cold and stony.
Love searches for spirit to invade a heart, warm and kind.
Spirit has a will and a way to keep you from being so lonely.
Gather yourself together and make that promise to be nice.

The real warrior has the heart of a child, because spirit is inside.
Inside of that innocent looking kindness beats the heart of truth.
No angry stony heart can possess or relate to such invisible light.
Let your anger and your fears subside to become a new you.

Walk with love and let time race into the future and revive anew.
Let your love shine forth and welcome those who love you too.
Pray with me now that all that spirit and all that love begins to move.
Let it change your heart and prove to all the world your real beauty.

Be wary of those who would steal your affections without being real.
They have words of sweetness and words of promise but lie in wait, hiding.
They tempt you with gold and physical beauty but later take and steal.
Guard yourself and lock away your heart to live in spirit. Live to be free.

Love freely in spirit and let God take his judgment on those who betray.
That same spirit that burns in your heart also gathers and burns anger.
Wheat and thorns live together, side by side, which in time God separates.
Live free, be happy, and love expecting nothing in return. Live forever.

by Cliff Rhodes
08/28/2007

51

ONCE UPON A NIGHT WHEN THE WORLD IS DIFFERENT

Though you don't think of your world as different, suddenly you find it is.
With love and friendship, rules and accepted norms, truth is soon revealed.
There is not enough genuine revelation forthcoming into this criticism.
You think I am different from you and that I dream of things unreal.

How do you know that love is you and that you already fill my heart?
Never once did you stop to think that a different door could open now.
Once upon a time that might have been true, so how it is now so hard?
How can things be different than the way you presume they are,...how?

You don't know me so why should I ever open that door and give in?
There is no evidence that your love is so different than a thousand more.
You've only just begun and I have never started to reveal myself within.
Love is pure and never dies so why should I worry if you never take form.

A thousand years have passed and so could pass a thousand more, no less.
Love will still be here. Why should I think only of this one moment in time?
I am not so important and neither are you so why would there be distress?
Be happy and our souls will meet again and be different if we find out why.

Challenge yourself to understand that we live together among spirits.
No one person is immune from love and no one should ignore the effect.
My dreams are my own and if I don't want to dance then I won't do it.
You open the door and find another dreamer and one day I may regret.

There is not enough revelation and not enough truth in this fantasy today.
Tomorrow is another day and there will be another night, or stay awake.
I will not be in your dreams and you will not be in mine, unless love stays.
I cannot say what love will do and you cannot make love forever remain.

Fly to another place to search for dreamers or make another try in time.
Your heart is too hard and stony for me to accept this situation as real.
God will see that you are a changed person and worthy of a loving mind.
God's love is all forgiving and forever available to lift you up to a dream.

Once upon a time we'll meet again, if even in a dream and we'll smile.
We'll know that we have talked and found a way to make dreams real.
Together we'll know that all hurt has been removed and love is divine.
Maybe then we can dance together, all night, or until the light is revealed.

by Cliff Rhodes - 09/01/2007

LOVE UNFOLDS INTO NEW DIMENSIONS

Love never lets go of new opportunities to unfold into new dimensions.
Whenever one door is closed another quickly opens and regeneration lives.
A spiritual awakening brings reflection of past mistakes and omissions.
She stands knocking at the door, begins a new adventure, and wins.

Catching that new wind of astral intimation gives me hope of new ideas.
Never before has there been such a strong beckoning of new worlds.
Out on the open desert of mental reasoning a new sea of vision redeems.
Far into the distance love beckons, lifting up my spirit to fly and soar.

Love brings again to mind and vision that surreal landscape of new hope.
Less than benevolent attachments bring disappointments to memory.
Friends who were less than friends grind into entropy with choices, so low.
Someone who has low expectations continues into the doldrums, dreary.

A fire of curiosity catches the heals of my interest and I run to the future.
Love is waiting to inspire me and I don't wait long to catch her hand.
She lifts up her feet above the hot dry sands of regret and wings unfurl.
I try desperate to hold on since she is flying with such urgency and so fast.

Above the past and present we roam, observing great egos and chaos.
There were some who never even had a heart to begin with nor kindness.
Why should I bother with those in such depression and disarray, such loss.
They don't even know which way to turn, looking within for more distress.

Memory is just a recording and can't be changed to regenerate minds.
She who was unique is now almost forgotten and not really lamented.
How long I had waited thinking something positive could be derived.
Now, I know it was not such a valuable adventure, never mind the rest.

There are no clouds ahead and no dark undercurrents of sadness that I see.
How real that love guides me again into new visions of hope and insight.
Love unfolds into new dimensions now waiting more abundant and free.
I see up ahead great hope and inspiration now beginning bright designs.

by Cliff Rhodes
09/03/2007

LOVE IS SPIRIT INVADING THE WORLD

Love does not need to be protected, since it overcomes all.
Love does not need to be safe and hidden, so you can wait inside free.
Your idea is not secret and spirit lets the world in on your loss.
You stay so afraid of your own feelings that you miss the great dream.

A sea of dreams is there and waiting only for you to launch your ship.
Open your heart to the world and the world will see your inspiration.
You have always been such a beautiful soul and comfort to listen within.
Speak what you think and write what you want, not in indecision.

Your mind is there waiting to thrill me with its broad brush and colors.
I know that your voice is there so beautiful and makes my heart glad.
Speak also with your clever intuition and your bright inventions galore.
I know I'll be amazed and there'll never be a dull moment and no sadness.

Why hold all that inside, still afraid of what people will think of this news?
You're not being directed by another and no one can keep you inside.
Let your spirit free with expression and let your love invade the deep blue.
That blue moon disappears with your smile and your wit and soon will fly.

Blue moon of sadness goes flying and gets quiet when love shines bright.
Your love is there and I've seen it invading the world, taking all by storm.
Forever you'll be a loving person even though sometimes it's hidden inside.
Open your heart to the world and sing of love and don't hide this time.

Love is spirit invading the world, never needing protection, not this time.
Love never needs to be hidden, afraid of anything, or anybody, not now.
Love should never fade away, nor shy away, nor wait, or even be denied.
Your love is a bright shining star that cannot hide its light. Now it's found.

by Cliff Rhodes
09/08/2007

TO PLAY WITHIN LOVE'S DREAMS

How can I play within your dreams, love, and dance upon the bright clouds
unless you catch my breath and my hand and lift me into your deep thoughts?
So deep and blue and magical are your thoughts that I am totally astounded.
You have remembered that I am waiting for just this chance to be able to
talk.

To talk in this rhythm brings notes to a background that makes beautiful
music.
Oh, how I long to just speak to you of little things, of day to day happenings.
To hear your response makes harmony in my heart of beats and poundings
too.
Since love so thrills my imagination, I see in you the blessed gift God brings.

Spirit is in you and rests but for a moment in my heart and then returns to
you.
Love knows you as a reflection and only sees in me a brief ache in my heart.
The barb of the arrow struck deep into my heart will not turn itself loose.
Love knows that if she takes out the barb that only my heart will be torn
apart.

She suffers me to ache so that I will live in spirit to return to her sweet dream
While I am sleeping, I wonder what the night's dreams will unfold into space.
Time and space separate into two different places where one is not so real.
The one I know for sure is real is the one place that I seek again and again.

I open that door this time and there is love standing pristine on the other
side.
Her dress sparkles in starlight, caressed by moonlight beams, now shining.
I grab my coat and hat and off we go, hand in hand to dance within time.
Hours and minutes go by and music makes a rhythm in my mind, now flying.

The room spins around and around and people are happy talking of light.
They speak of how light the party is now that love is dancing among them.
Flowers bloom in little green bowls on the tables next to candles, all bright.
Their yellow glow flickers on people's faces whose eyes soon are growing
dim.

The night is getting old and day will replace night in this land of time denied.
The last tune is played as the band finally plucks its last string on some guitar.
The last note is sung and the last refrain is hummed again, long and fine.
We're dancing that last slow, slow dance and I hear each note strike my heart.

Each night we separate and return to our own world inside of time, inside mind.
Dreams are only dreams but to play within love's dreams is so divine.
She calls to me and takes my hand each night to that place where starlight shines.
Catch my breath again, love, and take my hand and heart and I'll ignore the barb inside.

It doesn't even hurt because I know you put it there so deep where only you could find.
My healthy heart laughs when love plays her games and likes the barb just fine.
I'll never take it out, even if I could, because I know love put it there for just some time,
so she could wake me in starlight at night and take me to dance under the moonlight.
Dance with my heart, love and let it race, chasing all my blues away with your light.

by Cliff Rhodes.
09/12/2007

MIRRORS PLAY MEMORIES OF LIGHT

I saw her looking at the mirror to see what she could see.
Mirrors play memories of light and not what is inside.
They only play recorded messages that you see in present time.
What happened in the past so long ago and in our future dream?

How many lifetimes has that mirror recorded that you look at?
After you dream that dream, do you go back to the present to see?
Do you see again what was in our dream, the one we both dreamed?
Have you forgotten so soon, how in a dream we changed the past?

We meet again tonight and fly through time and fly through space.
Our future is not like the past so why do you have to return to see.
Everything is still as you left it, your brush and comb, right in their place.
You comb your hair so long and dark and I see such beauty and grace.

Does this continual return to the present comfort you so much?
You sit again at this mirror and think that some present life is real.
Yet, again night after night you follow me into the future of love.
You walk right beside me into the sun and into the rainbow and believe.

Why do we stay so close to each other in our dream of love and yet return?
You come back to this mirror to read what it says and see its image.
Day returns and we still remember our place, a moonlit night's world.
This mirror only gives reflections of your own world and not magic.

There is no magic in our dreams, only our love and we continue to dance.
This dance has no steps and no musical tunes that end in minutes, so soon.
Our movements are only beating wings that catch wind, moving so fast.
Fly with me love, and don't go back to that present, that mirror of moons.

Your eyes should look at mine and see how deep is my love and how real.
The love in your dream is more real than that light reflected in daytime.
I am in your dreams but I am not in your present life so why not sleep?
Don't stay awake; please go back to sleep, and take my hand and dream.

I'll see you on the other side where moons of planets lie suspended in time.
We'll fly through the galaxy and out to the edge of the Milky Way too.
Through the past we'll roam and when we tire we'll think of a future flight.
The present is not our destination though, since that mirror has only you.

I'm not really there so don't stay too long in time, standing still; I'll be blue.
Mirrors play memories of light, not movements of spirits in our dreams.
Stay with me now in this dream of dreams and sleep until light sets us free.

by Cliff Rhodes
09/16/2007

A MOMENT OF LOVE IN SPACE

Her wings brushed against my face and our hands barely touched.
I'm winning again and I stay happy for just this moment of love.
She doesn't know that she makes me so happy but it's hard to hide.
I can't exactly keep ecstasy a secret, since brightness is in my eyes.

I still don't know what to say and I can't imagine what we would do.
There's never any doubt that my mind is in a state of elation, so cool.
We couldn't talk and we may never walk, side by side, yet we know love.
Emotion is not just imagination and it takes love into a state of fun.

Love is an angel who spreads a circle of light into far reaches of space.
There is that place within our minds, a space, where love visits or stays.
How could I make love a constant friend and never worry where she goes?
Take me love, into your heart and never worry about why I need to know.

My heart is your safe place, your secret space where you can stay.
Why worry if I feel a need of emotion that is demanding or a drain?
I'm not one to put an emotional strain on your bright and sweet style.
Stay near my heart, love, and dream of sun and moon and blue skies.

We'll take our sail boat across the ocean while the wind is so breezy.
Why not let that strong wind take us both into the current of feelings?
Our emotions won't break and even if we both cry, we won't melt away.
We might struggle in our love and in our emotions, but we'll seize the day.

Happy are we who feel love and let our minds expand to take it all in.
God never said it would be easy but only that love would always win.
Love will rule our lives and make us rich inside our little secret space.
We never have to let love die or say goodbye to our spirit of grace.

Say hello again and again for I'll always be there waiting to join hearts.
Our spirits will fly together and unite in love and emotion in sweet form.
Love is an infinite spirit that will be here long after we both are gone.
It's my pure joy to share a moment of love in space, so you're never alone.

by Cliff Rhodes
09/24/2007

BREATHE AND HAVE FUN

Breathe in my spirit, love
and I will calm you at once.
Take me into your life today
and we alone will play.

Sleep no more in fear and loneliness,
since you have a friend to stay.
Watch the clouds and how they run away.
Now is the time to see what is best.

Lightness and airy moods make our day.
Don't stay in somber mind too long.
Take the time and find the best way,
to make happy times our own song.

Let me breathe in your spirit, love
and you can calm me at once.
I'll take you into my life today
so we alone can play the game.

Celebrate life today in spirit and love
and we can say together that we tried.
We'll make moods happy and lively,
take away all sadness, and just have fun.

by Cliff Rhodes
09/27/2007

LOVE HAS A COLORFUL SPATIAL ANOMALY

Flashes of light and sound mirror mental thoughts into being.
Pink lightning casts an illusion of awareness that is not real.
Touching heart and mind in one electric current still has feeling.
All my entire world resonates into one harmonic flow of empathy.

She looks like a myriad of fluttering, rotating around in rhythm.
Electric emotions emanate and charge the atmosphere of film.
A thin cocoon lines her outer body and she pushes to get out.
Reaching from inside her home, her safe place, comes her sound.

Sorrow and delight melt into one emotion and I find my way.
Light of day and peaceful night takes me into the same escape.
Love seems to be my redeeming and finds me again waiting.
Some day, all of the great energy of love will bring her refreshing.

She reflects my emotion into a whirlpool of nonexistence, apathy.
Although, pink lightning inside the sphere of recognition agrees,
she continues into that realm of enlightenment that brings joy.
Sleep brings to her dreams of enchantment, ending the dull noise.

My greatest heartfelt wish is to be a part of her world, her fantasy dreams.
Still I wait in mind, in heart, in mood, for some chance to rush into reality.
Dreams are so vivid and make some colorful spatial anomaly, yet unreal.
Small inconsequential things of speech and sight and touch bring feelings.

She thinks it is too much to become reality and wishes to remain in dreams.
Safety of her cocoon is of the utmost importance and soon I agree.
Never wanting to spoil the relationship, anything she wants is fine for me.
Soon the light will be fading and even the music will be only a memory.

Love makes friends so endearing but the spaces between recognition, sad.
One day there will be only one gigantic stream of reality and awareness .
Love has a colorful spatial anomaly that gives birth to new and rare dreams.
Blue green waters of the sea of reason and purple mountains of truth are set free.

by Cliff Rhodes
09/29/2007

LOVE IS A LONG AND WINDING ROAD

Suddenly, she found herself alone and in a strange place. It was a long winding road through darkness and in the middle of a deep green forest. She looked everywhere for a way out but could not find it. The wind picked up leaves in little swirls along the pathway, giving a further feeling of loneliness that was already dominant. After a few minutes of timidly walking along this forlorn pathway, it suddenly split into two roads. Which way should she take?

He wasn't aware that he was in such a desolate place and could not remember how he had gotten here. Storm clouds were covering the moon, the darkness was so thick, and he didn't know that the road ahead split into two different ways. For one moment the clouds left the vibrant moon and it lit up a feminine figure walking toward him along the path. His breath caught and both of them met each other's eyes for one brief moment. Suddenly, they were together even though they had not chosen or known each other's paths.

She began to sing a love song and his ears felt as if they almost melted with such a lovely sound. He knew at that moment, that this song would be forever in his heart.

Then he awoke from his dream, but the song was still on his mind and he had no idea who had made him ache with love so much for the joy of its melody. It was just a dream.

She woke up alone in the comfort of her home, and she thought that the song sounded right now, finally. She had been practicing it all week.

He wrote down the words to the story again and rearranged the adjectives and adverbs. He thought that maybe there was no moonlight, just bright sunlight. He still couldn't get that melody out of his head. Her voice was unforgettable.

She hit the high note again and sighed because she had a dream last night but couldn't remember what it was about, and that bugged her. Then she suddenly remembered, "It was about a circus and the clowns were so funny."

He was writing again and finally managed with good luck to get the subject and verb to agree. He thought to himself, "Writing is such a challenge. Maybe I should be an artist or even a singer. Now, where did I put that banjo?"

(I don't really play the banjo, just sounds nice, envious, but I did used to play the drums in a rock and not so rolling band and sing in my church choir.)

by Cliff Rhodes
10/02/2007

LOVE IS AN ADVENTURE WORTH RISKING PRIDE

The bright sun was hot as soon as it touched the horizon in the desert and soon became inflamed with bright warming rays of its medicine. Love was there because I followed her there into the desert and she touched me with warm sunshine on my skin.

The thunder began to roar and lightning flashed and clear pleasant drops of refreshing rain poured from the sky. I had followed love there and she held her hand to catch the rain. I drank from her palm, and when I had drunk all that she would give me, I kissed the kindness of her hands and wrists and I had no more thirst except for her touch.

Love ran into the mountains and I followed timidly after her climbing up and up and she carried me to trees filled with fruit and we languished there all the day until the night with sweetness on our breath.

Love left the mountains and ran to a cave, most deep and dark and perilous. I entered the cave and could see nothing only that I trusted love and wanted to be close to her spirit. On my last step that I would take, love pulled me from the precipice and falling backward I turned and fell into love's waiting compassionate arms.

An ocean began to wash over us, the water engulfed us, and I without breath and dying, fell at love's feet and soon began anew to breathe in rhythm with love's heart.

Love flew into my mind on wings of angels and saw my pride and asked if it would be there waiting to lift me to higher worlds of beauty and adventure and I cast pride out so that love could find me.

All night long I lay alone as one dead on the ground with only a rock for my pillow. With shivering cold and great loneliness I fell into despair. When I was deep in the pit of darkness, love came as if gliding on ice, but her feet were warm to the touch and her hands pulled me from the pit and held my face. One kiss and I was in heaven, her long dark hair flowing around me.

When the early morning sun peaked over the horizon and its bright warming rays healed like medicine, love touched me on my skin and I sighed. Then, love ran again into the desert, beckoning me, and again I followed her so that my beating heart would not be lonely for the heartbeat of love.

by Cliff Rhodes
10/06/2007

THE THREE WORDS

Words have no meaning in and of themselves
until meaning and substance and value are gained.
How can they be weighed and tested and remain?
They cannot unless two people decide to question.

I know why they were said because I said them.
Those three words make me feel good and well
as long as I meant the meaning I wanted them to tell.
Yet I question them only so I can find their depth.

I would love to know how deep those words are myself.
To know what reaction they made would be nice.
But maybe there is no feeling like I imagine to find.
Though I know who I wrote them to has deeply felt.

You have felt love so real and so sad and so joyful,
not that it was for me but still I know why you sing of love.
Once long ago or even just yesterday, you felt so deeply.
That is why I said them because I know love's extreme.

I felt the sound they made and I liked it and wanted more.
I wanted to know how much more I could feel,
to know how love visits one and not the other in form.
Or does it happen to both at the same time; maybe not real?

I would love to have an answer one day, yet that too is not real.
Just to feel the way I feel right now is good enough and true.
I hope you feel so much love for another that it sets you free.
Even in sadness you feel love that shows in your voice so blue.

Sing on, oh love, and tell us more even of love lost or love true.
I'll sit here and listen and even imagine I know what is real.
Your emotion makes it sound like it happened just today.
Whether it was someone else's song or not, your heart still dreams.

My heart dreams too and only sleeps when it has danced.
My dances are all with you in the night or in the day.
It's just play and imagination, but what caused those words to stay?
It's you, love, and not me and so many feel to be in the same trance.

Words on paper have some meaning but not enough to tell you.
How can they tell every thing that is felt in heart and mind?
The three words are not just blue or true or trying get through time.
They talk about YOU and say how beautiful YOU are and about truth.

I said them because everyone wants to but didn't, so I said it for them.
I'm so selfish and wanted to be the one to say it again.
I LOVE YOU.

by Cliff Rhodes
10/20/2007

THE SUN IS BLUE

Happiness is my emotion even I am blue, since love is happy.
No red bright Sun will do, since all the light is blue at last.
I see no reason in sight for that light to be any other color .
My mind is free at last to express my joy that love is real for her.

That blazing light is happiness beyond my imaginary dreams.
She says that love is returned to her and that makes her happy.
Since she is happy, then I am happy and resting inside this freedom.
I am free to dream again but free to remember too, the same past.

Once, back in time there was no love to be found, yet she gave love.
She didn't know she gave it, but it was shining brightly from above.
Her love was shining out from inside, yet all could see she was hurt.
She had been hurt before, and the pain showed an immense burden.

I felt her pain and wanted to heal her but I could not, so I waited.
Another knew how great and deep was her love and loved her back.
Now, all I can do is listen to the bright, happy melody played.
It plays for all to hear; her heart is no longer broken and sad.

Yet, still I am blue and feeling cold and alone as always.
I think I could be warmer in some far away place like space.
If I could fly, I would fly to the sun and hover around it in orbit.
Only there could I feel a little warmer, a little brighter; so be it.

My soul spreads its wings and lifts me into far away places.
I go out and beyond into the stars and into the great beyond.
I go out and around Jupiter, and Saturn, and back into space.
I yearn to be in the Sun, warming my wings in the molten pond.

I feel its warm, life giving rays, and bathe in its heat and light.
As I dip my wings into the molten gold, I turn blue from inside.
All my heart and my mind is already blue and leaking out.
Out comes the blue, mingling with the Sun's rays, shining aloud.
Still I am happy, satisfied that love has won the day, is found.

by Cliff Rhodes 10/28/2007

A NEW UNIVERSE FORMING?

Hum, shake, rattle, and roll, a new Universe is forming and love is to blame.
Today I felt a new feeling was moving around inside my spirit that took me
away.
I looked into the distance at some, not too distant future time, and envisioned
phenomena.
There was some new idea that began as a tiny beginning or only like a tiny
raindrop.

It bounced around and hesitated for only one second then morphed into a
crescendo.
Blending with air and space and meticulous memories, it reverberated
and haloed.
Each circle became bigger and brighter and began to expand into and
occupy time.
It permeated all existing dimensions around it and blended in with each one's
mind.

Not one could deny the presence of some different place of space and time
and emotion.
We touched each others' emotions and found a different idea than what we
had before.
No one suffered or became annoyed or became angry at the change and it
was welcome.
How can we not expand our awareness when love is present and both of us
can be reborn?

Are we not new people and not of the same, since the new Universe has been
born?
Yes we are new, and now we have more than friendship because as the spirit
passed through,
it picked up pieces of each of our own spirits and mingled them together and
made us new.
We now are not the same people that we were before we met and we have
been reformed.

A new Universe has formed, has expanded and welcomed us within its new
boundaries.
Still we reach to find its new limits but cannot because it has become so huge
within.

*Your world is beyond my imagination and I hope you see some new idea
within mine that was not in yours.
Sea, wind, sun and clouds, and green trees abound, but spirit is greater and
has made this a new Universe..*

*by Cliff Rhodes
10/29/2007*

GIVE A LITTLE HERE, AND GIVE A LITTLE THERE

All around me I find love and my breath is still inside of me.
I thank God for all of his mercies and all of the opportunities.
Around we go and we see on every turn that there is still love.
How beautiful and sweet are the dreams of those who look above.

See the wonder and the magic that unfolds at every turn in life.
We take a turn and just around the corner, we see the end in sight.
What will become of us when there is no more time to plan?
Our body becomes as the dust of the field and has no way to go back.

Will we still love when there is no more time or will we be out of the loop?
Around we go here on this Earth and chances we'll miss and cannot recoup.
How bright is the Lord's way and how kind are his steps to follow!
Let us be about the business of clearing away the rubbish of dreams so hollow.

Might we find some valuable investment and some great golden coin?
Or could we show that more worthwhile venture of helping another?
Which one will be heavier in the balances of life's poor miserable annoyance?
That event that separates skin from bone and sight from eyes is our only answer.

Dust will fly into the air and flesh will be no more, not even a fitting wrapping.
What will we cover our misdeeds with or what can we wrap around our omission?
Maybe we have omitted some great helping hand from our day to day working.
Give a little here and give a little there and that might cover almost all our sins.

by Cliff Rhodes
10/31/2007

DAYS OF TRUTH AND LIGHT BRING SAD EXCUSES

On death's doorstep rings the bell for us all and we try and find new inventions.
Love finds us looking for our new excuses, that we should have remembered.
Alas but we did not know ,or alas we did not see, such was a small and tiny decision.
Could we have felt some remorse for another human, or could we have been more tender?

Our feelings are our own, but we dare not let down our fence for even one moment.
Someone might think we care or they might even think that we could make a habit of love.
Give one small child a hand up or one old and feeble person a chance to invent.
They don't think to make some new engine but only to imagine they live another month.

Tell the truth about your feelings, that you have not cared enough for the weak and poor.
Let light shine onto your sins of omission and let the sun bring sad regrets of selfishness.
How often have you eaten and drunk your fill until there was no thirst or hunger?
Do you think that the old do not die of thirst and hunger in such a wealthy abyss?

They die at the hands of their loved ones who carry out their sad misguided wishes.
Love lives among us all our lives and we play and sing of love until the last days.
Then we think that to only sleep and dream is no life at all and deserves no chances.
So, we dismiss that tiny little world and that tiny little life as being such a waste.

We hate to see them suffer because we cannot talk to them any more or question.
They fail to respond to our questions or give vague and demented answers of nothing.

We think that they are in misery because they have illusions and do not think in our fashion.
Yet, do we know what they dream of or what light, God to them in their visions bring?

Are we so confident in our own relationship with God to think that we are so sane?
What is more a reality, to be overconfident and a failure in goodness, or only to be old?
If I could I would shout that the old and feeble still have life to live and time to play.
Their brains may not be looking in our direction or their words might not make sense.

I have seen them happy and glad to see their loved ones and glad to be with each other.
They love their sweet music, even though they get only occasional visitors and they breathe.
They feel the life go in and out of their lungs and they love the way sun shines even in winter.
Through their windows pour light and warmth from the sun, and love is only old memories.

I am saying goodbye to a lifelong friend ,who gave all that she could and loved everyone.
My mother is slipping from me fast and getting ready to fly to that other world of Jesus.
Weeks have passed so fast and now days and soon minutes will be all that is left to number.
Love gives evidence of its presence in so many forms, but none so rare as the love of my mother.

by Cliff Rhodes
11/12/2007

NEW TO ME TOO

*Love finds a space in kind hearts to breathe and live and fly to worlds
unknown.
Have you made some place in your own heart today for giving of
yourself and your time?
What would you do if love lifted you up and away to a place where
you're never alone?
Try as you might, there may not be a way to resist or turn away, or
turn back your mind.*

*New to me too is this surge of awareness, vibrating all the heart into
harmony and love.
How fast is the heart melted into pieces of caring and bits of affection
that stick like glue.
Mended, repaired, and stuck together is this new heart now ready
again for breaking up.
Broken it was and torn and shredded and laid to rest as a worn out old
blue moon.*

*That nightly light that illumines my sky, so dark and cold and blue, has
seen better times.
It returns again and I wear it as a memory that hangs about my
neck, mirroring my eyes.
That old blue moon never lets me wear it out, but keeps leaking blue
water inside.
I'll wager my pay and my old record collection that she never
transcends to the daylight.*

*It was a dream that mended my heart, took my hand, and whispered in
my ear, that rhyme.
Yet am I changed into light and love and perfect delight of reasoning
from spirit above.
Her songs and her sounds rhyme in rhythm with my heartbeat and take
me away in time.
Though locked in the night, she never takes flight into day, bright light,
and yellow sun.*

She rests in the night until dreams bring her out, now dancing and
singing all around.
No fair maiden could equal her company, a solace, yet moody and
yearning to be free.
This fading memory of light, sound, and ideas of golden relationships,
she now has found.
She knows it doesn't really exist, except in some space in time, not yet
of sound reason.

Her spirit flies into dreams and delights in appearing in the mist and
fog of some fantasy.
Yet no imagination is she to the mind, nor still again to the air, nor to
a reasoning moon.
So real is her hand, folding back her hair from a breeze that caresses
her mind, so happy.
She smiles inside her visions within her own dreams and says aloud,
"It's new to me too."

by Cliff Rhodes
11/22/2007

CHRISTMAS IS A DREAM THAT LASTS FOREVER

All you children should know that Santa is on his way soon.
He's popping popcorn for the elves and getting hay ready.
Hey, Rudolph doesn't know what popcorn is and the elves are busy.
They're all hammering and jamming away on their new tunes.

Rudolph doesn't eat popcorn and drink sodas, but the elves do.
How do you think elves work without a little incentive or play?
Mamma Santa doesn't' do popcorn or serve sodas all day.
She's making pies and goodies to keep Santa looking like a balloon.

He's got to stay fat so the chimneys get cleaned out real good.
If he jumped into a wide chimney, so skinny, he'd plop to the bottom.
Santa knows it, and Mamma Claus knows it, and you should too.
So, leave some cookies and milk and keep the fat man good-lookin.

Christmas lasts forever, but don't wait up to see the reindeer.
They'll be on your roof and away before the cookies hit the belly.
I saw him out of the corner of my eye one night but it was just a blur.
Red coat and britches and a big slurp and a gulp was all I could tell.

He's fast as a cat to be so fat and he'll surprise you with a smile.
That twinkle in his eye is almost like magic and so's the ho, ho, ho.
His laughter is catching and he'll laugh back at you in the night.
You'll know if he's caught you spying when you hear him tell a joke.

"To all a Merry Christmas and to each a happy night, now get back
in bed before I let the elves raid your refrigerator! If you think I ate
a lot cookies and drank a lot of milk, then wait till you see how late
your presents are if I quit feeding the elves popcorn and sodaz."

by Cliff Rhodes
11/27/2007

TIME TO COUNT THE DREAMING SHEEP

Love has a way of making the heart engage in seeking resolution of
dreams.
Taking spirit into a new realm of fulfillment soon amazes the
imagination.
Hope makes for an interesting life of memories and seeing the sites of
places so real.
Colorful mists of faded yearnings find communication with the
slightest notion.

A wave of the hand or the hint of a smile registers as agreement and
interest.
How can such insignificant, meaningless, gestures endear the heart
without thought?
Because some hearts have never thought to look for deeper meanings
or to quest.
Taking time to explore and to become enveloped in some relationship
seems just a loss.

Loss of control and loss of self is not worth the venture of spending life
in paradise.
But paradise is not real and therefore not to be sought after, except
only in idle time.
It is thought by some far better to be involved in the immediate catalyst
of energy.
Only fire can really seal a relationship and not thoughts of true peace
or joy.

Why bother with such a brave undertaking and consume all day in
search of the unreal?
Because some have truly seen the far reaches of the universe of love
and found it good.
Some noble adventurers have launched out into the deep of hatred and
intolerant ideas.
They have fought against narrow-minded isolationists who would
condemn any book.

Some sad souls find the unusual as abhorrent behavior and sweet empathy as a dull joke.
How could sleeping sheep dream of green pastures if the good shepherd did not let them?
Did God permit man to evolve into a higher sense of justice and goodness all alone?
I think no man ever went into this adventure alone and without some help from friends.

by Cliff Rhodes
11/30/2007

FOR THOSE WHOSE DREAMS LAST ALL NIGHT

The written words inspire to dream as if trees felt spirit in wind.
One small breath of communication has sway that's felt deeply.
How sweetly her words ring in heart and mind, so near within.
Flowers appear in colors and smells as if almost to taste the honey.

White clouds cover mountains of majestic beauty, covered in snow.
Suddenly, day breaks and layers of snow go melting and falling.
Almonds and all manner of fruits appear, revealed out of shadow.
Sunlight brightly illumines beautifully shaped valleys, now forming.

One lone bell rings and gives its tone of pure sound, telling of joy.
To one who was alone in darkness, there now is peace and breath.
How magnetic is that imagined place, within Earth's open void.
Deep in her heart there abounds some magical moving presence.

All across the waters are moving winds that stir and invite health.
Alive and breathing is this place in minds and dreams for freedom.
She walks softly and her feet barely touch smooth green meadows.
How often has liberty set free those in bondage who were as dead!

Dream on, oh people who wait upon love and spirit for a rescue.
She is not far away, and will visit on occasion those in real need.
Let not your dreams stop or be darkened with sadness or ruin.
Daylight within darkness surrounds and keeps faithful dreamers.

Love and liberty are one, the same, and comforts gentle friends.
Peace and love are free to those whose dreams last all night.

by Cliff Rhodes
12/09/2007

ROSES AND THOUGHTS OF JOY

Life approaches death, ever closer in circles as time draws near.
What remains to be seen is whether we have still our principles.
Breath is not so valuable as what we maintain is our liberty, ever.
Why compromise one breath for a minute longer? What does that tell?

It tells of truth as liberty has won and freedom cannot be taken in death.
Roses bring bright smiles, as happiness fulfills joy and new love.
Yet, liberty maintains its beauty, even when roses have no breath.
This present will sing louder and intone more clearly bells above.

Your thoughts are your own and no presumed love can take them.
Love and liberty are one and the same, and not mere infatuation.
Good rewards and favors bring satisfaction and ecstatic whims.
Still, you yourself know that if love is held in bondage, it's not real.

Happiness is a lie and contentment a cruel joke if liberty dies.
To be free of cruelty and criticism and free of hate is far better.
Love has no meaning if held in contempt and treated as a lie.
What you know is wrong yet holds you enslaved is not love, ever.

Free yourself and keep liberty alive, even at the cost of your own breath.
Love is liberty and liberty is love and never will one live without the other.
One had rather die without respect, without honor, or even alone in darkness.
The other will wither on the vine and be as dry as dust for a witness.

Let roses and thoughts of joy be for young immature women and men.
They think that attention and small favors bring happiness, then.
Cruel, temporary love holds no obligation to fulfill its bargain.
Without liberty of honor, and respect and freedom of thought, you cannot win.

by Cliff Rhodes
12/11/2007

HEALTH IS FOR YOU TO CREATE

Health is something that is made or lost or created anew.
The world around you is the one you make and contain.
Doctors and medicines are to help you to be healthy, true.
Though after all they have done, you are not free to refrain.

It is your world that you make and your health to keep.
Good health does not belong just to another; every one is unique.
Who knows you better than you? There is no one else to believe.
Building your health by making the world around you is a dream.

Not always is it possible to construct the perfect situation.
Though, there is one step, by one step, that can assure a change.
Start one day and then remember the next, shaping the fountain.
The fountain of youth and good health is not something strange.

Why blame facts of life like old age or genes or environment?
They all play a part, but if you're doing nothing, don't be afraid.
Today is the day to start taking control of your world and invent.
Write it down and decide how you want your world to be saved.

Pray to God to give you the strength and the will to find a way.
Though, you cannot change without making a beginning, to hope.
Where there is hope there is work and in beginning you awaken.
Your hope is work in itself and does not require even a loan.

If there is hope, there is work. If there is work, there is hope.
If it is beautiful, then it is truthful. If it is truthful, it is beautiful.
If there is justice, then it is pure and in purity there is justice.
All these things, done virtuously, bring praise not for you alone.

You are now changing your own world and mine too. Thanks.

by Cliff Rhodes
12/12/2007

LIVE LIFE TO ITS FULLEST AND START SHINING SOME LIGHT

So many people are always complaining and of a negative nature. How is it possible that they don't consider that to start an engine of beneficial thought, or a motor of positive thinking, and begin any journey of progress at all, that they have to begin with some good and kind hearted thing?

"He who is of calm and happy nature will hardly feel the pressure of age, but to him who is of an opposite disposition youth and age are equally a burden."
Plato, The Republic
Greek author & philosopher in Athens (427 BC - 347 BC)

Somehow I think that old Plato hit on a great note of positive influence with this purely enlightening philosophical idea.

I'm not saying that great teachers don't have their place like: a prosecuting attorney, or a great preacher who talks about the wages of sin, or the great mother or father who scolds their children to stay out of the street for their own safety.

Though, the real engine of progress and the goal of achieving a worthwhile, up to speed beneficial and enjoyable life lie in the initial formation of energy of expression that is positive and healing.

Have a beautiful and progressive 2008.

Cliff Rhodes
01/02/2008

SOME DOORS ARE ALWAYS OPEN

I was in my car the other day and a lady bug landed on the dashboard, within.
I caught her for to let her free but as I released her she headed back in.
She landed softly on my arm, and again I let her fly and let her go free.
The wind was not wild but the lady bug must have had a dream for me.

She flatly refused to fly but preferred to cozy up in a place, most busy.
I was trying to drive and trying to see exactly where that lady might go.
The spots were so beautiful and her wing covers kept vibrating like a bee.
But stay she did and she must have dreamed of making a home on my elbow.

I was weaving in and out of traffic and there was soon, a four-way stop.
Trying to be the respectable driver and preserver of all lives, I thought intensely.
The people won out though in the end, and I began to ignore her majesty.
Soon, back in traffic, there she appeared right on the mirror, a little red dot.

I wondered why she persisted to feel so cozy in my car, my life, my dreams, and my sanity.
So, I thought about why just a little royal polka-dotted bug should take refuge in my life.
She must have been struggling with her own problems, so I thought it noble to see her outside.
Stopping my car among the green meadows of the country, I let her have her vanity.

Gently I placed her between my big thumb and forefinger and lifted her up and over.
She was so light, and it was as if her weight was non-existent but real.
As I exited the car and held up my hand, she peeled back her covers and long tresses of silken wings unfolded.
She then caught a breeze that took her midstream into the tall grasses of life and again she dreams.

Never will I see that little replica of life, so tiny, but vibrant and significant.
Yet, she still dreams and she still breathes in some sunlit meadow, so real.
Why did she return to me again and again? I cannot say, but only God can.
Maybe one day I'll wish to return myself, to find the door that always stays an open dream.

by Cliff Rhodes
01/14/2008

LOVE OPENS THE MIND SPRING OF SPIRIT

Down inside the deep well of depression and loneliness, lies one candle.
That flicker is faintly felt and can hardly be seen except for its beauty.
The sweet beauty of so dim a light amidst thick darkness is unbearable.
Sweeping into a reality of sorrow and empathy I stretch my vanity.

How could I be able to see or even perceive this one that is so curious?
They fade into the background of noise and become only a distraction.
Death, Night, and Devil are so inept that they dim like fog into ice.
She looks in my direction as if some great angel has arrived in chaos.

HE came here once, and might still on occasion, if so moved to punish devils.
They have no heart to look him in the eye and me, they don't even notice.
I don't appear to have any power myself, but am accompanied by HIS will.
Sent here for the sparrow, we see it immediately among the rubbish.

As if on cue from some great machine above, the fires light up again.
No sooner than wings clear icy sludge, great flames soar up into space.
We have not wasted our trip and as soon as the sparrow is aloft, she sings.
Glory to God in the highest, and now I sleep in such a sweet, sweet place.

by Cliff Rhodes
01/31/2008

LOOK AROUND INSIDE CIRCLES OF LIGHT

To hold a sun inside your hand is never possible.
To hold love enclosed inside your heart is only temporary.
How that burden aches to display itself into reality!
Hearing and seeing and touching make life only partly visible.

That sun spreads its rays out through the cracks in your fingers.
That love beats from inside out and makes circles of harmony.
Become what you want to be and let your feelings search deeper.
Be aware of your inner child and see that you can change destiny.

There is no darkness that cannot be exposed to the light.
Nowhere is there impossible that cannot be overcome by possible.
All that is around you is being touched by circles of probable.
Allow the mind of your own skepticism to give up that ugly fight.

To have more faith and a stronger belief is a victory for you to claim.
To know that you are loved is so all encompassing and so surreal.
Yet, love gives you such a warm feeling in your heart and makes a flame.
Yes, there is a fire in the soul that burns away the refuse from its silver
surface.

Make this fire your own and let your heart of gold be exposed to hope.
Look around inside circles and rings of feelings to find that good way.
Even if all around you is bitterness and defeat, you can stay composed.
Even if total darkness is evident, you can spread light from a secret place.

Making a circle around in your mind and from your deepest being, it springs.
Shining inside your own sphere of reality it begins and becomes a star.
If where you are now is not of your choosing, then try to find a way to sing.
Happiness will soon be with you and your new way of hope will never be far.

by Cliff Rhodes
02/15/2008

LOVE IS CHANGING YOUR LIFE

Changing your life is making a positive difference in life's direction.
Love walks into your life and takes away your chaos, your entropy.
Why does she inspire to such extremes and lift up hope with fascination?
Never give up hope and love will find a way to make life a mystery.

She steps into the moonlight and reveals a mind of total beauty.
Her presence is felt by every person who is near her and we dream.
Unable to hold our minds in indifference, we intensely visualize her energy.
Sending dreams of fantasy and sweet light, she enters our reality stream.

What beautiful music, such romantic laughter, and so sweet is her voice!
My mind does not imagine another could ever be so perfectly nice.
She fades into mist too soon and I cannot find a way to again rejoice.
That silken dress that brushed against my hand keeps me thinking twice.

I think once about where she will appear next time the moon comes out.
Then I think about where she goes when the mists cover its bright surface.
The moon is covered now in somber gray and darkness is all about.
She hasn't let us see her reflection and it hurts to just turn my face away.

Her light will not play on shadows and dance with whispers, ghostly gray.
Yet I know that hope abounds and lingers, still waiting for love to show.
Love is like a magnet and pulls hope from deep inside the heart to race.
We gather our strength to wait so we can fly into that allusive glow.

Dark shadows have passed and love grabs my hand, quickly pulling me on.
She smiles this time again as if distant thunder is just a faded memory.
We take flight just in time before rain and ice make little drumming tones.
Soon there are no clouds, only feelings, and enchanting energies of peace.

by Cliff Rhodes
02/21/2008

BREAKING INTO THE OTHER DIMENSION OF LOVE

It matters not that you are in the other dimension but that you think.
How often do you try to find that other door and nothing appears?
Do you know that you have not achieved anything to look in that mirror?
Often times I see you in my mind and nothing bothers me as you blink.

You stare out and I stare in at the wonder and amazement of time.
Time has no season and no reason to pass, only that it gives results.
It brings proof of that jump in the continuum that we are sliding on by.
Surely and certainly we move from here to there regardless of our insults.

We say that we would have done so and have wanted to love but did not.
How many chances did we get but nothing arrived to break the entropy?
Not moving and not seeing and not hearing, we imagine what could be.
We insult the deity who made us by holding our hearts completely stopped.

Love is like a flower still blooming or a fountain still flowing and running.
When all the world is still and quiet and there is nothing, then who sings?
Who sings that song that makes our hearts beat faster or makes bells ring?
Take your chance while love is closer for she might be farther and leaving.

Waves of the ocean wash over our feet as we stand on the sand and wait.
The water does not stay but for a moment and the sand slides deeper still.
Soon the day will be cloudy and there will be no more time to be at play.
Clouds dim the daylight and night brings on the chill and love has no will.

Love waits not for the perfect day nor abides with us still as we imagine.
We might see the eagle or we might see the sparrow, but let her wings fly.
Let her lift you up, if only for a moment, so spirits will merge and life begin.
There soon is a new day and a new dream to make a new universe, in time.

Time waits for not one person, so let it begin with me and let me be alive.
Let me soon find a way to say all the things that are on my mind, this time.

by Cliff Rhodes
03/11/2008

WINGS INSIDE OF WINGS

Almost beating the air into rhythms of light and sound, they find their way.
Staying within my consciousness, I open my eyes and see the light of day.
There is no horror and no blood and there is only love for each reason.
The door opens and the curtain is pulled back to reveal a new creation.

Each new dimension is an expanding universe of light and theory and will.
The will of the mind has the opportunity to ride that wave into being.
Is there darkness, or the light of love that reveals a truly deeper meaning?
Horror has no place in this symphony of empathy, building into infinity.

Why stop along the way, peering into the darkness below, going slow?
Racing and surging and quickening, my heartbeat likes the speed of light.
Some strange feeling is coming over me and I feel that I am not alone.
A whole host of friends are there with me, along this journey, and smile.

She is my friend and says that the rain is but one drop in the endless days.
Navigating into this dream world of compassion, we find peacefulness.
Horror of horrors, there is no blood in dreams and no war and no hate.
Bullets fall from guns, harmlessly to the floor, and lose their vengeance.

Power is not eternally granted to the oppressors or the haters of love.
They quench their flames in the watery ocean of peace and find no hope.
Hope is for those of character and not free to those who force with guns.
Joking wildly, she laughs at the insane possibility of being free and open.

There is openness in love that flings wide the doors of happiness to flow in.
Let not sluggards delay our ascent into clouds above, so we keep our wings.
Wings inside of wings are revealed in the twinkling of an eye and it begins.
We start to see laughter, billowing up into real and actual rebirth of spirit.

Take upon yourself today, this day, this hour to invite love into your life.
Look through the eyes of spirit and let your heart be quickened, this time.

by Cliff Rhodes
04/04/2008

RECOGNITION OF SPIRITUAL LOVE AND MUSIC

The slight breeze gives evidence of the passing, perfume of jasmine.
At the same time, a friendly crosswind of gardenia thrills the senses.
Who was this creature and what name does she answer to when called?
What makes clouds form into recognizable figures that appear to all?

Memory is like a mist that smiles to those who bring back the familiar.
She was like that and almost like a friend, who left a happy memory star.
That bright light shines even after she has left and gone her own way.
Some friends leave stars and some friends leave sweet love songs that stay.

Swirling and revolving, light emerges into pure memory of delightfulness.
Reason and rhyme have no meaning when one unique color has changed.
It no longer has that pure and clear resonance that vibrates, as it once was.
Though, there it reveals itself in memory, it is suddenly in a new stage.

She now moves and weaves among new variations of light and sound.
Thinking aloud and humming a catchy tune, she now remembers too.
Playing that melody inside her mind is like seeing an old friend, newfound.
Tracing over the golden pathways, her spirit again ignites that wonderful tune.

Sound blazes and vibrates into some unimaginable perfume of harmony.
Gardenias go walking and jasmine takes off in flight with new sensations.
Music finds its way again into my personality and my spirit is happy.
What name does she answer to now that she has evolved into a new creation?

by Cliff Rhodes
04/08/2008

FLYING IN THE COMPANY OF STRANGERS

Close your eyes and imagine that lightning has just hit your location.
You are now in the process of gathering speed and lifting off from Earth.
You are not in a spaceship or even in your own car but sound asleep.
You have now entered a world that you are not prepared for and have
never been in before, but you are too late to escape, so you relax and
pretend to just enjoy the ride. No turning back since you are, of course,
asleep and you wouldn't stop dreaming now anyway, because you want
to see where this dream is taking you. Passing low over pine trees and
then barely above the lake, you make it to the foothills of the mountains
and begin to climb. Who is to the left and who is to right of you? They are
friends that you have met and talked to but have never actually seen them
in person. Your garments are making rustling sounds as they flap in the
wind that is passing by. Only it is not just the wind because it is you who
are moving and faster now that you are lifting up over the mountains.
Far below, nestled inside of the broad mountain range, is a small group of
buildings and nearby is a river. As your body settles down, you see in
front of you a rough wooden house, huge with a long front porch, and
then you and your two friends approach and then knock on the front door.
Inside there is music and laughter and all around the forest is the smell
of fresh pine needles spiking the air into wintergreen and you breathe
in the clear fresh air. Someone opens the door and there in front of you
is a roaring fireplace with many friends gathered all around because
there is a slight chill in the air. Hanging as if suspended in mid air is a
chandelier in the middle of the room and each person looks into each
others eyes and then smiles. Your friends are happy to see you. Each one
tells a story about their own lives and then you tell yours. You cannot hold
it inside and the very descriptive tale emerges with all of the accompanying
metaphors of what has happened today or yesterday or maybe from the last
year. Each detail is recorded in the mind of the group and everyone agrees
that what happened was very unusual to say the least. The beautiful blue
vase on the mantle is impressed upon your memory and you wish privately
that you had one just like it at home. The windows are open to the front
and snow is piling up on the lawn and now two doves have landed on a
window sill and stay but for a moment as the wind chases them into a
warmer place away from its chill. The music has started again and the
same melancholy songs merge into the familiarity of the evening and then,
.....you awaken.

by Cliff Rhodes 04/13/2008

SEARCHING THROUGH TIME AND REASON -
(TWO ASTRAL PLANES RUNNING SIDE BY SIDE)

An array of spirit self leaves evidence as emerging light transfigures time.
Not willing to stay long, escape into a further atmosphere of being begins.
Yearning and willing to emerge is how feelings and longings find new life.
How many days have you been waiting for someone's hand as a friend?

So often we wait too long until there is no heartbeat and no wind inside.
Breathing and opening our eyes, we start to wonder why there is no way.
We must open our hearts and our minds if this road opens up into space.
Barriers, gone now, the future unfolds into layers of opportunity and light.

What was that memory that brought on reminiscing so soon, this time?
I don't know how it happened but I recall a division within the night sky.
So many of the stars were divided and half were emerging into daylight.
The other half were there as if hanging, suspended, and waiting in the night.

Darkness was enveloping a chance that we might have had, then silence.
Then, as if magic, the spatial plane of some astral phenomena opened up.
Why were there suddenly two pathways instead of one, feelings of love?
We both felt love and that should not have been, changing our innocence.

If one just felt love for the other, then that would have explained it all.
Yet if the other felt love and one did not, then that too would not be a loss.
So time opened up its melodious comedy and we entered into its mystery.
Here we are trapped; not going forward, not tracing our steps seriously.

Though we don't care either, love has traveled this path, always with us.
We don't want to forget and we still don't want to remember too severely.
Love is such an honorable emotion that it brings all harmony into being.
Side by side, here we are and going in two different directions, in love.

There is nothing requested of this state of being, except to just exist.
The thrill and the ecstasy of a continuous state of bliss are not so bad.
I can read a book in this state of mind or if I so please, just be still.
Reality is there too and empathy and fear and sorrow, but not so sad.

I remember you and your songs and they bring me such joy and happiness.
There are now more of us and we continue our recordings and memories.
We play back the sites and the sounds, so that they stay familiar to senses.

Two astral planes, running deeply into time and reason, maintain my bliss.
One thing is very sure. No one owns love and love visits whom it chooses.

My dreams may not be yours and your dreams may not be mine.
Who knows whether or not two different paths diverge, then circle into
infinity?
Love will still be here when we have all gone away and visits in its own time.

by Cliff Rhodes
04/18/2008

OPEN HEARTS AND OPEN MINDS MAKE NEW MYSTERIES OF LOVE

Mystery of mystery unfolds and there is no ending to the bottomless pit.
How your heart wishes to see love in any form but still there is no reprieve.
There is no future and no past and you are stuck in the doldrums of self pity.
Why cannot some wayward spirit fly down and rescue you from no feeling?

You want to feel some remorse and feel relief from loneliness and torment.
There has to be some hope and some light that shines into darkness alone.
Far away in the green meadows of deep thought you hear a song of hope.
There is happiness that makes inroads into your desperation to begin.

Light plays and dances on a tiny drop of water that is clinging to a leaf.
You focus in on the visualization of this green meadow in far away fields.
Once, you remember that alone you were walking and a vision appeared.
You felt the breeze brush across your face and kiss your cheek, adored.

You knew that my thoughts were with you and I reached out to you again.
I couldn't find you any other way except to send my dreams on the wind.
I transmigrated through station after station of endless eons of time.
Circling and revolving round and round, I waited patiently to arrive.

I am not who you think I am but I am more than you will ever know or see.
Your love has arrived to again take your hand and let you begin to feel.
Change will begin slowly and then we can together walk those green paths.
Let my soul brush across your heart's tears of freedom and happiness.

We will open our hearts and our minds to the sunshine of peacefulness.
Together, we will fly away from the bottomless pit of hate and pride.
Our witty inventions of laughter will make our hearts merry with lightness.
You and I are now together again, dancing again, talking again, alive.

by Cliff Rhodes
04/21/2008

WALKING THE EARTH IN THE PRESENCE OF SPIRIT

Why do we think that we have lived here so long on this Earth, alone?
Sprit is with us now, as in the beginning, but we are not like spirit.
We are born, we live for a short time, then we die, and spirit goes on.
The rose itself is unsurpassed and makes a splash of beauty for the eye
within.

Though bright red roses are not easily forgotten, they soon disappear.
We are exactly like the rose or even a beautiful tree that doesn't stay.
We walk the Earth for such a short time but spirit too is very near.
Let that spirit live in your breath and remind you that you are never alone.

You are not making your way unobserved and unattended, solely to exist.
Everything you do is being observed and watched and measured by God.
Wait! Why are you so worried now, because he's here as in the beginning?
We will all go away soon and vanish and it is not important to be in shock.

Spirit tells us that we are more than just flesh and blood because of love.
We are more now than the rose and more now than the tree or the grasses.
Love is not a part of our molecular makeup and cannot be taken back.
We cannot take back to ourselves that which is not of our own, an enigma.

Love is of spirit and spirit is of love and meanders in and out of our lives.
We do not own love any more than we own spirit and now we all laugh.
We are so curious that love intrigues us because we realize it lives.
Love lives after us with others and goes with some of us after death passes.

Can I say of my own self that I am the one who loves or is it spirit within?
I say that it is spirit and love will still be here when I am dead and gone.
My bones turn to dust but that spirit who laughed and smiled was of Him.
He it is who walked the Earth before you or I were imagination alone.

Let us rejoice that He will see again the rose bloom, year after year.
His spirit will walk the Earth, inspecting the flowers and observe the rain.
The slight breeze caresses His roses and His children again and again.
Love will visit the people of the Earth and stay awhile if they draw near.

Love cannot be taken or killed or even deterred in its path to freedom.
Skipping across the spirit of the people of this land, love visits one by one.
Each is special and deserves no less attention than any other, it seems.
Though whispers are vague and words make dreams, Love seeks Liberty.

Where liberty echoes along great valleys and huge mountains, love lives.
Walking from one end of the Earth to the other, love lives with spirit.
In spirit is freedom and liberty stakes its claim on love and freely breathes.
Fill your lungs with love and adore the spirit that lives, forever free.

by Cliff Rhodes
04/25/2008

CONTINUOUS PAIN

leaving	The locomotive was leaving.
pain	The train of pain pulses free.
serenading my	It was serenading my senses, divine.
my soul	My soul was living, flying in time.
my heart	Caressing my heart, love speaks.
my emotions	She has taken my emotions into dreams.
running quickly	Wheels make sparks, running quickly.
through my veins	Spirit engines ride rails through my veins.
revolving	The smoke of love is a revolving train of pain.
around inside	Screaming around inside, electrons take charge.
taking laughter	A network of synapses are taking laughter too far.
making joy	They are making joy an emotion of their own.
continuous	Light of electrical emotion is continuous and slow.
nonstop ecstasy	A staccato of visions give nonstop ecstasy.
pain of reason	The pain of reason creates ideas of fantasy.
my joy, my mind	Love is the engine of my joy, my mind.
her presence	Her presence makes me ecstatic, frightened.
I look around	I look around and see jewels of gold.
inside	Inside the engine every shadow is broken.
a box	There finally is found a box made of diamonds.
the walls	The walls are brilliant, creating illusory light.
are a vision	You are a vision, a non-existent creature.
breathing	Pain creates flames of familiar breath.
we are breathing	We are breathing inside each other's minds.
so afraid	I am not so afraid, because I feel safe.
of the pain	She is the author, the writer of the pain.
so welcome	She is so welcome to cause me to dream.
the feeling	How does it all happen, the electricity, the feeling?
to exist	To exist is to live, to breathe truly free.
inside	Inside of the inner spirit there is a train.
we are mind	Wheels turning wheels, we are mind today.
together	Together the mind is aflame in continuous pain.
tomorrow	Tomorrow we change direction.
destination	Our destination is now salvation.
unknown.	We separate and find a new unknown.
creation.	The new creation is not you or me, but soul.

by Cliff Rhodes
05/04/2008

FIGHT

Fight is a generator, an electrical infusion of energy, fueling delirium.
Conspicuous glee from being in the jet stream of power gives
supremacy.
Inability to change direction leads to defeat and betrays interception
of momentum.
Getting your attacker off balance, rewards with a fierce defeat of the
enemy.

FORGIVENESS

Forgiveness brings healing and ability to grow and learn about your
own mistakes.
Concession to harmony brings rewards that can never be realized
without grace.
Infinite peacefulness gives satisfaction and amazing realization of
truthfulness.
Being in the spirit of honor and wisdom rewards everyone and brings
self respect.

FRIENDSHIP

Friendship springs into being newborn and generates quality of life
and invites love.
Breaking down all barriers of confusion and chaos, love lifts up mind
into heavens above.
Spirit permeates all objects and transmits ideas and feelings across
infinite distances.
Leveling power to the lowest point of energy, love overcomes all and
creates balance.

by Cliff Rhodes
05/07/2008

THE TONGUE IS TRYING TO TELL TRUTH

*The tongue is a magnificent beast that gives form and substance to my
words.*
*I use it to change them into shapes and syllables and raspy consonants
that hurt.*
*I lash out in anger and also in sweet, almost silent, whispery rhythms
and beats.*
*I make the ears of my receptors feel each and every intonation, so that
they believe.*

*They must believe that I am here and that I exist and that I am a real
person too.*
*How can they think they are my friends unless they truly believe that I
don't sleep?*
*Wake up tongue and tell the truth and say that you have twisted words
so crude.*
*You are the enemy of my soul and also my savior when you tell
convincing stories.*

*Please, artfully twist and revolve those words around my lips so that
even I believe.*
*If only I am convinced that I am real, then so many others would see
the same as I.*
*They wouldn't doubt the validity of my tales of valor and poems of
lovely beauty.*
*Try again and bring into the air those ideas that are burning within
and let them cry.*

*Let my words unfold like velvet tears into the innocent ears of my
readers to be moved.*
*Maybe they will be inspired to speak when they read of such brilliant
exasperations.*
*Could it be that their tongues too will tell the truth as I am now telling
so cool?*
*I doubt it could be foretold so soon that they would be renewed, in
their condition.*

99

They don't have to pry and lift their tongues, contorting words into devious expressions.
Many already know how to avoid that burning and simmering truthful spirit of love.
Some have become familiar with lies and deceits and darkly moving tales of oppression.
Me, I swear today to begin to be a better person and keep my tongue on the word above.

Knowing full well that to only try is a miserable failure; I will surely fall to the ground, slain.
Let me not give up the ghost until I have at least mostly told the truth, one or two times.
If you are reading this tale of the tongue, of lies , and of terrible consequences; be afraid.
I am the one who told you and warned you that your tongue too would be better off, silent.

by Cliff Rhodes
05/08/2008

TO BE RELEASED FROM YOUR OWN PRISON

I am remembering that I, myself, am not the reason for being a real person.
It is that spirit that has accompanied me all along my way through life.
Through the night and through the day and all along the path, I see love.
Fights and strife and deepest thought-provoking reasoning will not inspire.

Have you ever believed that inside that void there is a spark that heals?
Somewhere inside that greatest of open panoramas of emptiness, there is light.
To be healed is not the main objective but to receive forgiveness, freely.
Is it easier to say get up and walk or all is forgiven and open your mind?

An open door is an open pathway so why even have a door to be opened.
The reason is that to some it is hidden and to others, who choose, revealed.
No one can force you to walk in this direction or make you have hope.
It is your own choosing; to look for a different way or find and believe.

Time passes by and sun and moon continue to make their circular paths.
Night and day passes and clocks are ticking slowly but surely, ironically.
Youth grows and passes and then the body is informed that it will not last.
Not long now, hair is getting gray, and wrinkles are forming, inevitably.

Your allotted time on this Earth is leaking gradually from your great life.
You have had your chance to choose a different way, not the way of death.
Life is healing itself and mending its broken and torn spirit, all the time.
Even as a body loses the conflict and loses the contest, love has breath.

Love breathes inside your spirit its healing medicine and all is forgiven.
You live again and live forever inside the spirit that moves the waters.
As great waters are flowing and tides are turning, so is your inner spirit.
That great void is filled and that yearning is satisfied with extreme resolve.

Let your hopes become evidence of opening and swinging wide that door.
Your choice is now becoming clear, reaching out, and slowly turning as before.
Life is changing and rearranging, your greatest expectations, taking form.
Never have you known that you were living inside your own prison, bored?

Your soulful heart cries out that it needs love and wants to be healed, freed. Let your heart be released from its own prison of need and dream of calm seas.
Join me as we fly over the surface of the ocean and sleep in sweet dreams. The quickening is awaiting your entry and waits for your knock, patiently.

by Cliff Rhodes
05/11/2008

I'M STILL DANCING - I

In the night there is a light divine.
It chases my mind and finds delight.
No brilliant sun shines to make tired eyes.
Another dimension is waiting, nice.

Flowers open to moon's hypnotic trance.
Enchanting sweetness spreads fantasy.
Hours of pure elliptical dreams are passing.
Don't turn out the night! I'm still dancing.

Vision's sweet nectar stays nightly adored.
Silently, mental screams engulf two storms.
Both inside different dimensions are torn.
Two minds disappear, then take form.

Memory is not present only a presence.
Nothing to control, all is lost to essence.
Too late to un-dream the dream, incessant.
Merciful love has overtaken and is unrepentant.

Why are you afraid and feeling out of control?
The same music is playing as shadows roll.
Reflections on the walls are moonlit contortions.
We are nonstop evolving into one distortion.

Two games played and only one game won.
Don't turn out the magic until we see the sun.

New daylight springs through windows fantastic.
Why are you asking? Of course, I'm still dancing.

by Cliff Rhodes
05/11/2008

103

I'M STILL DANCING - II

In darkest night shines light divine
to find delight and chase the mind,
no brilliant sun to tire my eyes.
Other dimensions wait inside.

Flowers open to moon's night trance,
enchanting, sweetness, fantasy.
Hours of elliptical dreams pass,
music in mind. I'm still dancing.

Vision's sweet nectar stays adored.
Silently, mental screams contort.
Two storms inside, dimensions torn.
Two minds disappear, then take form.

Memory only a presence,
not in control, all is essence.
Tis too late to un-dream the dream,
love overtakes, unrepentant.

Are you feeling out of control,
music playing as shadows roll?
Reflections on walls, contortions,
evolve nonstop, one distortion.

Two games played into one game won.
Passing magic soon sees the sun.

New daylight springs, now fantastic.
Are you asking? I'm still dancing.

by Cliff Rhodes
05/13/2008

HAIKU:
5 syllables
7 syllables
5 syllables

To The One Who Loves

Racing, racing, heart
Love has finally found you
Take your time to think

Loving Sleepy Summer Days

Sleepy, sleepy, head
Don't wait too long for coffee
Summer is passing

Love's False Summer Sleep

She sleeps soundly now
Summer's flower opens full
Winter's howl is gone

Imagine, Mending Broken Hearts

To imagine is not to be saved.
From above, on high, is the way.
Thinking that to be free is to feel,
feeling that a memory is real
dreaming doesn't bring you truth.
Truth opens the door for life a-new.
Make your way to have faith.
Without faith, all light is faded.
Afraid and alone, still there is hope.
Hope leads you to see the ghost.
Your soul is about to be changed.
Change is all around you, rearranging.
Take some time to think.
Your troubles are not you, sinking.
Sinking your ship is not winning.
Win by lifting up your heart.
Hearing the Word will take you far.
Your own words are not so real.
His Word, has real meaning,
here since the beginning.
The Word brings life, takes away sin.
Love is all around you, look again.
I am the worst of the worst,
broken all the commandments in my heart,
yet, saved from sin and hurt.
Walk with His spirit.
Watch yourself change within.
Breathe in from the Spirit.
Live life with love and friends.
Jesus sees you near and far,
making new dreams, mending broken hearts.

by Cliff Rhodes
05/26/08

Outline For Mercy

Seiza, a position on the floor, on bended knees,
with the tops of your feet
touching the floor,
while sitting on the heels
is quietness, tranquility, inner peace.
Love, merciful love, in its unmercifulness,
is not touching lightly, but soaking
its respectful follower in
the maelstrom of its vortex,
falling with vertigo into infinity.
Screaming that you could
never be angry in love's presence
because there is no respect of persons
gives you hope that you
might live through the event.
It is a reflection of your loving soul,
that you have nurtured
and cared for through extreme
tribulation that you can never forget.
Why would you tell such lies
as if the words were so sarcastic
that the reader could immediately
tell that it was not your nature?
Yearning for love, you invite
the event to return as if your
imagination could fuel the spirit
of any believer who might
stumble upon your precarious situation.
You perch along the outer
extremity of the vortex of

love's magnetism, hoping that
your nonchalance and avoidance
of direct contact might insure
your salvation from love's
inevitability.
Then you fall headlong
into your imagined experience,
struggling to survive when you
could become enraptured
in love's wide open doorway,
communication.
Self pity, self deception, alcoholic trance
of denial and retribution for
the unwillingness to give back
or continue friendship is not quietness,
but noisy chaos.
A never ending friend is tranquility,
golden nirvana.
Self expression,
release,
breath is inner peace.

by Cliff Rhodes
05/29/2008

Love Is Deeper

Deeper and deeper we sink into oblivion, trying to find Love.
We continue on, full well knowing that it is possessed of mystery.
Trying so desperately, we know of its incredible fantasy.
Under the ocean and above the clouds we fly, looking for fun.

Trapped by its appeal and burdened by its demand, we risk exposure.
Fun and fulfillment are not so costly as to cause love to abandon us, no?
Where is the beauty and where is the end to loneliness that was so sure?
Love promised me to stay close and always be comforting my soul.

She cries that love was here now and in a moment is vanished into mist.
Looking into the mirror, she sees only loneliness and abandonment.
One small tear has managed to leak from empty eyes to appear as evidence.
Heart break and sadness and that pale horse plays into visions of torment.

He has finished his seeking now tired from such exasperation and toil.
She cannot be found in the air or under the sea and he has looked endlessly.
Such beauty she possessed and she captivated his heart like no other joy.
Where could she have disappeared to and left him clearly in a void?

We argue in the night and no longer see in each other the magic once clear.
I know this person next to me but no longer is it who I once thought.
Visions upon visions, memory's first meeting of the minds still lives forever.
Dreams now in confusion and lover's first thoughts now turn distraught.

Is my first impression so divine and then deeper feelings reveal truth?
Love is an ocean of mystery and a deep unfolding of voyages in time.
We pass through many doors and beginnings of revelations to get through.
Each one must now stand alone and seek their way until the time is right.

Communication is divine and compromise sublime if it brings togetherness.
Loneliness is not the end of the line but only a beginning of contemplation.
Thinking is a companion and a comfort is memory if depression will rest.
Let not your hearts be troubled, who give their minds to love's devotion.

God sends divine wisdom to all who seek love's comfort and companionship.
Time will pass by and there will come another to win your heart and mind.
One cup will empty and another one fill as long as your spirit is willing.
Love is deeper than the ocean and evolving deeper than you feel this time.

*Next time will be another chance to try and find within yourself, true love.
.........true love, to give.*

by Cliff Rhodes
05/ 30/2008

The Sword, the Mirror, and the Candle

So long ago I learned the way of the sword.
My sword, folded steel, made by forging,
has ten times the strength of one thousand folds.
No foe could stand before my mighty blade, so bold.

I wielded it for a fair maiden of the truth.
Her bright beauty was so immaculate in youth.
Now she tells me to look within my own soul.
See if you can find any fault not of gold.

My mirror I polished clean and light is sharp.
Its reflection never slows from my heart.
I see within all errors and all misdeeds.
Humbly I calm my spirit, seeing reason.

My love sees my soul and my inner energy.
She turns away in angst at my new words.
I now have so clear that soul but no good deeds.
Where is my light to shine forth to be seen?

I take my candle inside my mirror clean.
Its light and smoke blacken my inner me.
I yield my sword to break the glass.
Sword and mirror fall free, shattered.

Now my candle shines forth from me,
giving light for all to see.

by Cliff Rhodes
05/31/2008

Clown for a Day

The day started out early about 5:00 A.M. when I got up and started getting ready to be a clown for the Hamasa Shriners Big Fishing Rodeo. I laid out my clown uniforms that some great people had given me and others that I had bought or made. It is better to just make your own from brightly colored cloth if you can get someone to sew for you or do it yourself. I sat down in front of the mirror and began to put on white paste first, all over my face and ears and neck. Then, I accented my eyes, and mouth, putting colored lines for big smiles and wide eyes. There is a special setting powder that makes it stay, so I used it because this was going to be a hot day. Next, I opened up this little plastic bag that had a bright red wig stuffed tightly inside and out popped this gigantic red wig that looked almost as big at a sombrero they wear down in Mexico. I thought at least it will keep off the bright sun and be somewhat of a shade. Then I put on red socks, baggy pants that were cut off with suspenders, and a brightly colored shirt with short sleeves. It was going to be hot and was a sure thing. Then, I loaded up the car and tore out for north central Mississippi and the Noxubee Refuge where the lake full of catfish waited to be caught and pulled in.

I received some great gawkers and lookers from people I was passing and meeting. They just stared at and gazed fixedly at some crazy guy with a red nose, gigantic red hair and multicolored face full of wide grin.

I made it to the location but not before passing and weaving around potholes and plain out tire breakers at various locations and I think I was almost the first one to arrive at the ranger office. The nice lady in the parking lot gave me a stare and pointed to the right and said to turn right and go about three miles and it was on my left.

Just in time I got behind the big Shrine van and followed them down the road to the turn off. We arrived tuning right once more onto a dirt road off another dirt road and there was the lake or lakes. They looked as if the fish had purposefully stirred them up from the bottom and mixed mud to color the water an even brown color. Other vans and trailers started to arrive and my partner, in his clown getup soon arrived too. Tents were already there and coolers with cold drinks and ice and odds and ends needed for sun protection were brought out.

After a bit, the beautiful children started arriving. Some of them were escorted in wheelchairs and others walking bravely on their own with crutches or walkers or artificial limbs. The most striking detail was the way they walked with integrity and forcefulness, giving no ground whatsoever to any seemly little handicap that was going to slow them down and waste their precious time from their destiny to catch a large catfish. The artificial limbs were synchronizing themselves perfectly in their hypnotic movements, making first one then another limb move almost as rapidly I walk normally.

"Hi, my name is Squeegy. What's your name?" I stuck out my hand and held tiny little hands that were first a little bashful, then brave and forthrightly loud eloquent voices told me theirs, one by one, leaving me thrilled that I had such a beautiful experience to meet them, face to face. I am convinced that bravery comes in the smallest and the more frail packages, direct from God, just to show us non-handicapped people that it is He, and not us from whom the bravest hearts are attached to. The brightest smiles and the most cheerful attitudes were from the handicapped children with their little eyes in total wonderment and the thrill of waiting for the fishing to start.

Soon, one by one they spread out in little groups along the pond, out next to the water. I felt a duty to walk along the edge of the lake with fan in hand and personally make breezes, rustling the strands of hair from the small heads of these most special guests and cooling them off one by one.

Eventually the cry was heard, "I got one!" The net man soon had to help them to get the really big ones out and they were very large fish by any standards. I've caught some fish in my time that would completely fill up a frying pan by itself, but these biggies would almost fill the whole oven. When they got one hooked, the water would boil as if some big monster was trying to get all the water out of the pond in one big splash, with just his tail. Sometimes the parents and other Shriners would help to get the really big ones to the side of the pond. Big eyes and big smiles and yippies and yays and out right screaming with a child's wonderment filled and echoed around the trees of that magical little pond. Someone told me that the catfish had not been fed for a couple of days, so they would be hungry and believe me those catfish were hungry. Some of the fish had to be left inside the net and lugged back to the tent to be cleaned and put into individual coolers so the families could carry them home to their refrigerators.

For approximately one hour and a half, in sticky hot sunlight, there was sheer pandemonium, alternating with complete joy and outright fun. I was going from one bright hot little face to the other as I fanned the children with my little fan and made slight breezes rustle their hair and as I told them I was going to mess up their hair with my cool breeze every one said, "Yeah, that feels really cool", then their was suddenly an exclamation, "I got another one!"

We soon packed up because of the heat and loaded up all the kids and went down the road a little ways to a shaded pavilion where hot dogs and hamburgers galore were already cooked and waiting. Prayers were asked for God to bless the food and the hands that had prepared it and the food to the nourishment of our bodies and our bodies to his service and still asking for more blessings for these wonderful children. Prizes were given out and trophies to every child, even if he did not catch anything, and comic books and each one received a huge applause for his fishing ability and perseverance. Proper recognition and credits were given to those that helped. Then, we packed it up and headed back to Meridian or other areas and towns in this part of Central Mississippi or beyond.

I arrived back at my house and took off the clown stuff and rubbed off the makeup with mineral oil and then got down on my knees and thanked God that I had the chance to participate in one of the most beautiful things I have ever witnessed in my entire life. If they told me that I would have to give up an arm and a leg to continue being a clown for the Shriners, I would say go ahead and take both of them because I would pay it if I had to, just for the experience of seeing such joy on those children's faces.

A friend of mine told me a year ago that it would bring tears to my eyes and he was right.

by Cliff Rhodes
06/07/2008

Wait for the Night

Spirit
Breath
Love

The body auto-relocated

Wherever the body is
There will the eagles
Be gathered together*

Love is intertwined into
Spirit

Love is so sorrowful
And has such pity upon
She who is so sweet

Please don't burn up
All the oil in your lamp*
Leave some for the night

Spirit will come and visit
In the night
The terrible, cold
DARK, Night

I will visit you in the night
I will be your breath
I will keep your heart safe
In the night

I will not let the talons
Of the eagle tear you
Nor the claws of the lion
Rip at you

I will keep your heart
With me
In a safe place

Wait.
For the night.

*Mathew 24:28 For wheresoever the carcase is, there
will the eagles be gathered together.
*Mathew 25:03 They that were foolish took their lamps,
and took no oil with them:

by Cliff Rhodes
06/10/2008

Medieval Retribution

A wealthy proprietor says to his young apprentice, "I dare say my good man! What in heaven's name caused you to grieve the Count so and move him into such a despicable attitude, this time? You know full well that he is one of our major clients and to whom we at this establishment serve in no less than four different venues!"

"Sire, I did but glance at the young woman's bodice, though not for more than the briefest of moments. She did entice me sire, with her eyes and with her hands. She placed her index finger in just such a position, upon her lips as if to say, that I should not speak. I did not say a word to her, sire, on my honor as a gentleman. It is sheer folly for his royal excellency, the Count, to accuse me of conspiring to meet her in private."

"Son, as of this day you no longer have a job at our establishment. Take your leave at the start of the afternoon. I mean no later than when the shadow of the sun has crossed the line of the North Star, on the equatorial sundial in the courtyard, or I shall have you flogged! Take also that stray canine that followed you here, which you have been so fond of, or I shall have the wenches who beg for food, butcher him for their supper. Be gone from me!"

Thomas had not eaten for the day and did not even know where his next meal would come from. He gathered his sparse clothing and decided not to wait until noon, but rather would leave hurriedly before the proprietor returned from his hastily arranged meeting. The indignant man had gone to apologize for the actions of his young apprentice. Thomas left by the side door into the alley and just as he was leaving, one of the cleaning wenches happened to be throwing out a bucket of slop from the upper story. Her raucous laughter echoed off the alley wall as the foul mixture covered him and the stray pup. The young canine yelped but Thomas didn't even flinch, only hung his head. The day was not starting out very well.

He shuffled down the cobblestone street, being careful not to step in the sticky brown patches that clung to his meager sandals, as it would be difficult to clean his feet without proper water. He and his puppy traveled not more than the length of a furlong, with him looking constantly down at the street. To his surprise suddenly, he saw directly in front of his own feet, two other feet incredibly more beautiful than his own, and rising up from those thin delicate feet was a long flowing white dress. When his wide eyes fixed a steady gaze into the beautiful young woman's eyes, he quickly put his hand up to shield his frozen thoughts.

Immediately he dropped to one knee and did not even lift his gaze from the young woman's feet.

"The Lord will surely strike me down because of my terrible bad luck at being forced to look into your eyes for the second time today."

She let fall from her white gloved hand a delicate brown leather bag and when it hit the street it made a metallic sound as it was full to the brim with gold coins.

"Take the purse, go to the Templar at the bank, and tell him that you want to open an account. Say that you would like to keep only so much as necessary to purchase a horse, a new suit of clothes from the tailor, and a sword. Meet me tonight at the courtyard when the moon is full. If I don't see you, then I will assume that you do not agree with our arrangement and I will promptly find another. You smell like a pig"

As she turned away, the hem of her dress brushed across his face.

"Could I at least know the name of she who has redeemed me from the terrible situation, in which she also placed me, because I did but gaze into her beautiful blue eyes, and did momentarily look upon her immaculate bodice?"

Glancing back, looking directly into his smiling eyes, she said, "My name is Christine, and hurry up and pick up the pittance of gold I left at your feet. Oh, and by the way, I brought it back from purgatory. The Lord Christ who lifted me from that terrible place has seen fit to make it duty free, with no strings attached. It may soon disappear though, so you better spend it hurriedly. All of Saint-Trond is looking at you, kneeling in the middle of the street."

"My name is Thomas and I love you, your ladyship. I will see you tonight at the courtyard in the moonlight, after I have bathed, no less."

"Bring your script, young man. We have much to say to these people."

by Cliff Rhodes
06/12/2008

Here are two web sites to research the life of Christine of Saint-Trond if you are curious. My writing is purely fictitious, as you might have guessed, except for her name, the name of the city, and an intimation that she had returned from purgatory.

http://monasticmatrix.usc.edu/commentaria/article.php?textId=3234

http://www.crwflags.com/fotw/flags/be-vlist.html

This is my interpretation of the day that Christine and Thomas first met, with a little romantic twist. First off, I am not Catholic, but I have an ecumenical marriage and have attended on regular occasions at several different Catholic churches at the request of my wife. She also has attended my Protestant Baptist church when I could convince her to. It is a sad commentary that we Protestants do not make historical recordings of special people who have been born, lived, and died in the Protestant faith. There have been far too few who have actually left a historical record but there is no doubt that they have left a great benevolent influence on their congregations. The record has been left in their hearts but insufficient care has been taken to actually write down what actually happened in our protestant churches, though miraculous, and supernatural things have occurred.

Christine of Saint Trond, is said by many historical accounts to have died, resurrected, returned from purgatory and made many unusual observances, even bizarre, if conceptualized, among her friends, family, and the public at large. At her funeral, her body is said to have revived, risen to the rafters of the church, and after she returned home to her family, her body took on many transformations and accomplished many unusual supernatural phenomena. During the remainder of her life she converted many to the Christian faith by her preaching. This is highly unusual for a woman to have done, especially in a male dominated Catholic church. There were many women in the Bible who served as great teachers such as, Miriam, Deborah, Huldah, Priscilla, and Phoebe. The churches today would be at a great loss if there were no women teachers who helped to spread the gospel of Jesus Christ.

Shifting Light on the Other Side of the Mirror

waiting for a breath

now in another minute

no, almost there, next

who was there?

guessing it was you

because I know

you are the one

who waits for me

to go to the other

side of the mirror

so many times you

have been there

in a dream or

in my vision

of how it could be

so pleasantly better

than it is now

but you are not there

 except only

out of the corner

of my eye

in an illusion

where the light

begins to shift

in the deepest of sleep

when there is no chance

that things would be normal

as if it was in the daylight

of bright sun

nobody knows

what is in there

way behind the mirror

on the other side

of the mind

that prevents us from

seeing what we see

late in the deepest

dreams of our

surreal mind

that nobody ever touches

because if we see it

we wake up

so we will never remember

and we never remember

ever, ever, even if it

was a dream that we

never wanted to leave

so tell me that you never

sleep or never dream

and I will laugh at you

because when you do

there will always

be something that

will make you wake up

so you will not remember

even if it was on the

other side of the mirror

that you think is the

reflection of your

own memory

you lay down and

begin to remember

the day and it flashes

across your mind

and then you forget

that you were remembering

things from the day

and you start to open

the mirror of the mind

and it is not just a memory

and it is not just a reflection

you pass through

across that bridge

to the other side

of the mirror of the mind

where the light is shifting

and you are in the same place

the same as me

at the same time

by Cliff Rhodes

06/18/2008

Dreams from the Mirror of the Mind

lightning flashed all along the sides
of the mind sphere
and when it would occur
it was as if it lit up the back
of my eyes and ricocheted
all through the brain

I was dreaming and entering
the place I never knew
that I would remember

because I had never
returned to the same
place, but only through
another way, a way that only
you can remember since
you were there too

we both saw each other
in the vortex
and then emerged into the
river of life,
an unbroken
line from the beginning of time,
stretching through the years,
like sand through our hands

thoughts and ideas ran together
and I didn't know which ones
were yours and which ones
were mine, but we both knew
that we were together in
a moment in time, frozen

the point of beginning and
the point of departure
were both here
in present form

ecstatic ripples made
known by the inability to
summon the courage to leave
but neither one wanted to

light was not from the sun or the moon
but from an almost incandescent
presence of two souls, bound into a single
point of love and breath and life

entering into a silent dimension
that neither one could leave
until they were both awake
at the same time

by Cliff Rhodes
06/25/2008

When Love Visits Do You Want To Survive?

In my mind there was a ghostly quiet before the storm.
Then it began to build as visions took the place of memories.
I was quiet when it first began and then gradually I became tense.
Dreams began to seek the boundaries of my thoughts and there was a door.

She was waiting, just on the other side, and beckoned me to enter.
The path was clear and my steps were aright and I did not hesitate.
We crossed over to the other side and immediately took flight, taking turns.
She was my guide and then I was hers as we reached, finally the pathway.

Lightning flashed all around, tingling our skin, and both of us were exposed.
Electrical current charged the synapses and memories became one.
Her thoughts were my thoughts and our memories blended into a river, flowing.
Would I die at this point in time and never return to the daylight, I imagined?

The exposure was so severe and so overpowering that I wasn't sure if I would live.
No means of escape was offered for my safety and I questioned why I was here.
Could I survive the entry into the surge of awareness that she was leading me within?
All previous memories were nonexistent and I still wanted to venture further.

She and I challenged each other to stay until the end, until everything subsided.
We waited, not knowing if either one would live and return to the daylight, to awaken.
Tormented by each other, we held on until the light returned, the light of the night.
Electrical light was all around us and we finally passed through the vortex and were safe.

The moon glow brought welcome shadows into every part of my dark room.
Its shadows seemed like old friends compared to the electrical light of the dream.
Darkness enveloped me and brought me comfort with a soft light of blue.
I was awake and looking outside into the street and I was temporarily free.

Tomorrow would be another day and also another night to seek and to find.
Would she be there with me in another dream or would there be no one there?
I hoped I would not be alone again in the night, but if I was, there was always time.
The next time that love visits, I hope to survive as I did last night with her.

I think we both were hoping that neither one of us would be lost in the vortex.
That streaming surge of a hurricane made all who enter, mere passengers on a ride.
We held on for dear life and hoped and prayed that we would survive the test.
Sometimes love is patient, and sometimes merciful, then at times love defies the mind.

by Cliff Rhodes
06/22/2008

Night Visitor

Thunder and lightning flashed across the dark night sky and she was there waiting just behind the tree line, out of sight from any would be observers. The back of his house was bordered by a fence that was covered in vines and young bushes, that had grown up from lack of trimming. The grass had not been cut for weeks and there were high weeds all over the yard. She felt like she was safe in her hiding place, behind his house but yet next to him, as close to him as possible. She had never gotten this close before, and the thrill was bubbling up inside of her because he was actually inside this house. She could see him now, walking back and forth in front of the curtain in the kitchen.

He was beginning to prepare a late night supper of whatever can his hand had landed on from high up in the cabinet. He spun the can opener around and emptied it out into the small boiler that was just big enough to hold the contents of the can. He was thinking about her and how far she lived from him and all the things that she had written at the web site. This woman, this young beautiful female, was writing about her needs and her emotions on her web site. How interesting she had found the attraction of love in just words and sentences. Her words had hypnotized him into writing a similar type of pros and poems and the two of them, constantly read each others writings and emailed back and forth. He looked out into the night through the kitchen window and rain began to patter on the leaves and patio tiles in the backyard. It would be great to meet her face to face in some quiet restaurant or cafe for a candlelight dinner, just the two of them.

She was growing impatient now and waiting for him to turn out the lights and go to bed so she could enter through the broken lock on the window. She had casually and conveniently broken it when she passed by during his lunch hour earlier in the day, and no one had been the wiser.

He had finished his meal of carrots, peas, and tuna fish, all coming from a can but fast and good. He drank iced sweet tea from the refrigerator and then slipped into his bed with not even the sheets covering him. Everything was nice and cool on a warm summer night and no need for anything else.

She had become soaked from the rain and was tired of waiting in the hot humid summer night and wanted so much to just take off her clothes and step into the shower. That would come after her work was done. She read his poems of love and laughter and wrote her own in response to his alluring appeal to mirror her own emotions in his words. They were such trite little poems that he wrote and his work would never be famous or even reach the desk of the publisher. She would make sure of that tonight after she had finished what she came here to do. First, he would be surprised to see her and she could just imagine the look on his face when she entered his bedroom and put the gun next to his head. She was going to take out her knife at the last moment when he was completely enraptured in her beauty, and had absolutely no resistance to her overtures.

He was finally able to rest, laying sprawled in the bed and completely relaxed. His eyes were closed and he was thinking of her and the beautiful poetry she wrote, giving herself completely into the emotions of the words and expressions.

Click!

"There is a bullet in the chamber of this 357 magnum and if you scream, yell, or jump, you'll be dead. Relax, I'm not going to hurt you. Just relax. You know who I am."

She jumped up on top of him and they both kissed long and deep. She let the pistol slide out of her hand, carelessly, and it lay useless on the bed close to the other pillow.

"The next time we play this game, you're going to be the one who breaks into the house and stays half the night, outside in the pouring rain!"

The dull end of the huge butcher knife raked across his throat, then fell with a thump and a clang as it skittered across the floor and hit the night stand.

"Yes, dear."

by Cliff Rhodes
06/27/2008

The Day of Dawning

Morning sun is cresting the horizon and bright light is all around
My eyes look full into the sun and on this day, I am not blinded.
One day soon God may come and take away my spirit and I shall fall down.
Into the ground my body will sink and nothing will be left but light.

What I did for others will still be left as an essence of my solitary presence.
I drew a map for some wayward stranger to find his way and helped him home.
For some poor beggar I gave what I could and he drank and dined in elegance.
The church bells rang as I was leaving one day and I felt fine in my soul.

I left words of happiness and sorrow so people could feel something in their hearts.
They were void of emotion and from me they shared my misery and my joy.
Some poor child laughed because of my insanity and my mirth made him feel smart.
I relieved some dread burden from a long time friend and made his debt a void.

I could have cried for my misery and anguished over my financial condition.
Instead, I laughed at my misfortune but celebrated with God, my good health.
If I could eat from the finest tables and drink the finest wine, I'd be in derision.
No decision will ever be more important than the one I made as a child of twelve.

Wealthy or poor, sick or healthy I'd put my trust in the Lord and walk his way.

I'd try my best to fit my footsteps into his footprints and make his pathway mine.

No force on Earth or in the Universe could make me change directions or fail.

I would hold on until the end, until heaven opened up and I saw the cavalry of Christ.

If my bones turned to dust and my lips parched dry, I'd still wait to thirst not.

That life giving water is the word of God and only his word could part the veil.

When the curtain was torn, we were all given a chance to go directly to God.

Wait not any longer but ask and it shall be opened and free you shall be and saved.

Now leave something of light to be carried on and think back upon their faces.

Maybe you will see a memory of some good you have done or even a small favor.

If someone is in need, then pass it on and surely it will come back around in a day.

Let not the sun go down upon your anger but let it arise on good deeds and faith.

by Cliff Rhodes
06/29/08

Independence Loves Freedom

He wasn't asking for any more freedom than was necessary to do his job. He was a killer and had a target and that was all that mattered. Should he consider the target was cold or hungry or had a family or feelings? That didn't matter and the target was a non entity, a no name piece of crap that wasn't going to make a dent in this entire world of madness. This target was a piece of paper and only the ink that was used to write his name on had any significance. Today was the 4th of July and it was a killer's Independence Day as well as America's. This shooter was going to be independent from working a regular job and independent from having to take orders from anybody except a computer moniker that gave him his targets.

Sunlight played dances on his scope lens and that bothered him because he didn't like light messing with his job. It was as if he had to fight sunlight as well as pull the trigger. The car was coming into view now, around the corner, and the killer had set up in a fourth story window of an abandoned building.

The driver of the car had the radio going and was thinking about the freedoms that we all have in the United States from oppression. How beautiful it was to have God on your side and spirit moving in all directions at all different times into all different dimensions. Do we know what great things that God does for us and do we really know the mind of God?

The killer was about to have his independence day celebration begin. His finger was on the trigger and moving ever so slowly as his target was about to pull up to stop behind another vehicle at the red light. Light again reflected into the scope from some unknown source but managed to penetrate the killer's eye at the last moment. He pulled the trigger and his target was hit. He witnessed it with his own eyes and soon his bank account would be full again and his freedoms would be preserved for another year. Targets like these only have to come around every once in a while to let him play in rich resorts for a whole year.

"Independence loves freedom," he thought. "I can choose to live the life I want and nobody is going to stop me from doing what I need to get rich."

The light also glinted into the eyes of the driver and for a moment he couldn't see even the vehicle in front of him. He put his hand up to shield his eyes and then he saw through the cracks in his fingers that the traffic light had changed to green. He pulled the sun visor down and gave the old car a little gas and went on toward his destiny.

"God is truly a miraculous being," he thought. "God is full of varied dimensions and thoughts, if we can call them thoughts, and he moves one mountain in front of our eyes and exchanges it for an ocean, at the blink of an eye. Independence loves freedom and God is independent of any time and space that we live in and is free to do what ever he wishes or wants with our lives."

The gas gage was nearly empty and surely he should have run out of gas before now, but he doesn't. Soon he sees the sign and pulls over at the next gas station. The meeting he is going to will spark a new generation in energy and give Americans the independence that we all want. Independence loves freedom and all of this energy should be free, just like that sunlight that shines down on us right now. His little invention was lying in a cardboard box on the back seat of the car and had the letters, FREEDOM, scribbled across the front of it.

by Cliff Rhodes
07/04/2008

I Told You Not To come

You came to visit me again.
I told you not to come.

I said that I would see you
and you knew that I would.
I told you that I would talk to you
about all the things you wanted.

I said, "Don't ask me to say it."
You asked me to say it
and I said it, over and over again.

I told you that I would tie you up.
You also knew
what was going to happen to you
when I did
and it happened,
over and over again.

That was the way you wanted it.

There was nothing gentle at all.

Everything was gentle, so nice.

First, I was bad, very bad.

Then I was good, so very good.

I hit you but you said it didn't hurt.

I threw you in the floor.

You were still tied up.

I stood over you and asked,

"Why do you come to visit me?

I told you not to come.

You should never come to visit me.

This is what will happen to you."

I gave you a spanking.

I made it hurt and you cried.

With trembling hands,

I brushed the hair out of your face.

I took my fingers and wiped away the tears.

Then I kissed you and untied you.

I said, "Don't ever come back.

You know the same thing will happen again.

I will do the same thing, every time.

It will happen over and over again.

Then I will kiss you

and wipe away your tears.

Don't call me and don't talk to me!

I don't want to see you again!

If you really want to talk to me,

I'm here any time for you baby."

by Cliff Rhodes

07/05/08

Deep Cuts Heal, But The Price Just Keeps Getting Higher

The lights were completely out and the back yard was pitch black. I had forgotten to leave on the outside light. I fumbled with the keys and could not find the right key to the gate. I would have even more trouble with the house keys. There were two more locks. Diminished light from a far away street light was my only savior. First, I opened the bottom lock and then the top lock. I finally managed to open the back door and put my hand on the sword that I left propped up at the inside door frame, when I heard running footsteps behind me. With one hand holding the saya and the other the textured grip of the katana, I managed to withdraw the sword and swung out and up to meet the downward strike of the pursuer. How he had found me, I didn't know. I turned and began making counter strikes and defensive blocks with the sword and sparks flew up into the jet black night. All I could see was an outline of a human form and he was taxing my strength to keep his attacks from slicing into my body. Sometimes I couldn't even see the strike coming but I felt it and the whistle of cold steel cutting through the air. Back and forth we fought, striking, paring, and thrusting into the black night, neither one permitting the other to make a mistake. On his last strike he made a weak off center attempt to turn his sword into my exposed neck. I used the extension of his arm to hold him to his committed strategy. The valuable second it took for him to recover gave me all the time that I needed. I blocked and moved and let my sword slice behind my turn and felt flesh and blood give way to the sharpness of my blade. No sooner had I cut cleanly across his stomach than he also turned and managed to slice at a glancing blow into my right thigh. I knew I was cut but not so bad as he was. He faded into the night and I managed to get into my house before I heard the gunshots. In my minds eye I could see the area surrounding my house and could sense that the danger was over, temporarily.

I live in a bad neighborhood but it is close to where I work, so I like to walk to get the exercise. Sometimes I think that it would be better to drive to work and pay the high price of gas, but then it is just going to get higher and higher. Anyway, I would just get sedentary, sitting in a car all day.

by Cliff Rhodes
07/05/2008

You and Me Again

Faster and faster my heart is beating and my feet are pounding the street.
Why do you think I am running except to outrun destiny and time?
I go out five miles and back five miles making ten in two hours easy.
But it is not so easy if you quit and never remember because habits will die.

Is love that way, if not habitual, suffering and dying if it is neglected too long?
What agony do you have in mind for me if I don't think of you or write?
You know that I have dreamed, will dream of you again, and sing your song.
I cannot stop from taking you into my life and my reality, yet still I cry.

I have my tears and my aches that creep into my whole being, unashamed.
They occur in the darkest hour in my night and before my daylight comes.
After all the running and the practice I begin to feel a backwash of sameness.
My physical labors do not bring an end to the wanting and the desires of love.

Sometimes tears are for sadness and sometimes for the agony of wanting.
Do we all have this deep abiding want to be something we are not, still?
What if there are no tears but just a tremendous need for her face, smiling?
Dreams and apparitions appear in a moments notice at the first loss of will.

There is no sadness now and still yet no happiness, but she is with me again.

She's in my mind and my heart and all of my being and I cannot stop to think.
Pictures of the present and the past are floating by and those of the small ship.
She was sitting there and waiting for me to enter the water, but I didn't go in.

I am drowning in a sea of emotion and apathy too, without an end to reveal.
I didn't want to say that there was love because want and need are not real.
The mind is a cruel regulator and takes no prisoners in its quest to reason.
In a dream may I steal a moment of your time and say words so truly needy?

I saw you and I need you now and I feel your presence always in my heart.
There are no words that could express these lofty feelings that never leave.
I can never quite get you out of my mind and I will never be out of the dark.
It is you and me again, waiting for the moon to turn its shadows into dreams.

by Cliff Rhodes
07/08/2008

Time Dilates

Time almost never opens up to let in the momentary casual observer.
Every once in a while, time unfolds its velvet wings and gives
audience.
You need to properly get yourself transported with correct visual
words.
Never must you doubt that this phenomena exists, but
let faith transcend.

The vortex is there waiting for you to enter with the ease of a dream.
Your mind is the engine of your valiant efforts and must always be
free.
Let your mind free itself from the tiring toils of the day's stresses.
Give up that problem that keeps you Earthbound and be released.

Now we are reading about time past, time long ago, and all is in the
past.
We are going back into the past when the people of the book lived.
They walked this Earth, sometimes eating and sometimes fasting.
Gathering their wood, they made small campfires and cooked their
fish.

Time was recording it into the rocks and onto the sand, imprinting
itself.
Love was also there and would be remembered by time itself, being
etched.
It was scratched into the fabric of the universe and is ageless forever.
Love is an eternal spirit, springing forth forever, newborn expressions.

First love is imprinted into the universe of memory and will never die.
Ageless love will be flowering over and over again in hearts and
minds.
Never dying and never turning brown with age, love is eternal light.
Your love and my love is recorded through time and remembered by
time.

All of your deeds and misdeeds will be forgotten and never remembered.
But love, first love, ecstatic love, and forever love will reach into the future.
Lovers will remember that it existed because time will tell them in pictures.
Time is not alone in this conspiracy because all the angels keep the embers.

The fire burns eternally and will not die out as long as someone is in love.
Love is not of your own, but is part of all others that has entered the flame.
Some burn brightly, then simmer and die, while others continue from above.
From some lofty crevice in the mountains of memory, past loves engage.

They meet in the clouds and look down upon crystal seas of blue and green.
Circling around in a vortex of delight and fantasy, their hearts are beating.
Past lovers are reborn, living again in wispy clouds and snow white beaches.
They visit each other to remember the love they had and cherish its memory.

Time dilates yet again and takes them back until a new love has been found.
Then the reunion begins again of all love and all lovers in eternal memory.
Ageless and timeless, love springs forth yet again, playing its magical sounds.
Music and happiness abound and time finds another lover to record its fantasy.

by Cliff Rhodes
07/10/2008

The Train That Waits On Time

Waiting at the train station, she thinks back on where she has been.
Was it really love that took her away from her home and brought her here?
Why did she leave her family over just a picture on the internet of him?
Never could she imagine in all her life that she would be held, forever.

She walked in that day expecting to see her Love, her Dream, her Angel.
Instead, she found a Devil, and he was so cruel that she couldn't imagine!
Her mother's face still appears in her mind, telling her to be careful.
How could she have been so crazy to trust this person she had never seen?

The train should be here any minute and she doesn't care where it goes.
It might go to Boston, or Atlanta, or anywhere but here, only quickly.
The nightmare should have been finished, but it still repeats over and over.
Darkly she remembers that it was a shock when she was captured by him.

He never gave her a chance to scream, only to cry inside the mask.
Her mask was fitted with a device to let her breathe, under his control.
For some reason, she thought that he would let her leave, when she asked.
The pain was not the worst, but the fear, and the other things, unspoken.

Her eyes are still inside the mask---footsteps, heart beating faster!

by Cliff Rhodes
7/14/2008

Love's Dark Clouds Bring Rain

Ominous and forbidding, love's dark clouds shout angrily, closing the door.
You are my lover and my friend but now say that you don't need me anymore!
Why were you so coy and so nice and never once told me you would leave?
I never ever thought you would love me and leave me so cold and asleep.

I cannot wake up from the dream of a perfect reality that made me feel real.
I was a new person and no longer dead from the old and the dead and dying.
I felt like a new creation, molded and formed from your mind of bright light.
Dark and dead was I and not even awake but shaking and cold and freezing.

I saw the dark, cloudy, silhouette form around your beautiful shapely body.
Yet, I could not agree with my reasoning mind that you were a shadow.
Oh, I lied to myself and told the world you were real and not just madness.
I was left flying high and weaving in and out of lofty clouds at the top.

But, then you discovered that the world was yours for the taking of any love.
You saw that love was your oasis and gave you to drink from its fountains.
The water flowed over you and adored you and the clouds were mountains.
They were like your lovers arms, surrounding you, holding you from above.

Then they began to grow ugly and threatened me with their presence.
The dark outline around your pretty body began to howl and get angry.
Suddenly the sky opened up and love was not what I expected of her essence.
She began to pour torrents of rain from her dark clouds, loving me madly.

by Cliff Rhodes
08/14/2008

Love's Sleepy Assurance Again Granted

Death is not so final as to dislodge that assurance of peacefulness.
Way beyond comprehension from only a fleshly mind, sleeps love.
She is passive and quiet and does not prepare for a war of willfulness.
The hand that has taken and prepared the soul does not release any blood.

There is no knife and there are no cuts along that thin line of rebellion.
Freedom has reached the end of her chain and only she can fly truly free.
Those who have not the chain reach almost to the sun and crash and burn.
Yet, love and freedom are tied together with a tether, almost unreal it seems.

Wait, but I know this condition and am not privy to explain any further.
For I am at my wits end to see my own chain of freedom coiled below me.
I look and try with my greatest anticipation to feel it yanking and hurting.
My wings are so strong and I have left even the Earth and expanse of seas.

Now teleported I am above my own body and observe its peaceful sleep.
The third person spirit has granted me a view into reality and beyond.
Sleep on myself, deep within that dreamy sleep of lovely sweet reason.
She still brings me joy and informs me softly of the limit at which I stopped.

I would have gone further and further upon that rocky road of retribution.
But still there is the hand that never lets me stray beyond all
reasonable means.
What barrier is this now that is invisible to me and my ultimate convictions?
Why it is the road to sin which I travel upon and participate in regularly.

I am such a sinner and real low life scoundrel, but I even I am free to fly.
Sufficient to stand but free to fall, I stop short of being burned by the sun.
Love has kissed my lips and felt my passion and now I sleep again inside.
Sleepy assurance has again been granted from the compassionate one up
above.

by Cliff Rhodes
08/16/2008

Vacancy of Love, Vacancy of Soul

There is a vacuum where the soul used to be, that spirit, that love.
Horror of horrors, there is no soul any more! But why did it leave?
Where is the guilt that should plague my mind and put me in agony?
I wish there was such guilt that I could cry out to some god above.

I am a reasonable person though, and I cannot make such a mistake.
I think through every little event but this is an unusual problem.
There is vacancy in my being and my synapses are not firing the same.
How can I restore the proper balance within my human body chemistry?

What could bring my nervous system to such aberration, such anomaly?
I am as one lost who does not know his way, and how can I explain this?
Maybe sin, that phenomena that hurts myself and others is a true reality.

What if there is a chemical reaction corresponding to my actions?
My body is not impervious to my decisions and my life choices.
Now that I have lost my very soul, I have no sense of direction.
How can I get it back; how did it happen; where is that still small voice?

by Cliff Rhodes
08/17/2008

The Time of Changing Love

Doors are open, lights are on, and there now is a new path to follow.
Heart is ready, mind is sharp, and thoughts are about fantastic hope.
Come with me into the new dimension and realize your greatest fantasies.
You never will have to wonder about your ultimate destiny, your last stand.

The sign of the cross is there in the clouds and shining forth for all to see.
Sunlight sparkles upon the cross piece and two different ways seem to meet.
You have chosen the way of the cross and it surely leads home to family,
the family of God and the family of man and changing love for all eternity.

Love is changing now from a self centered humanistic specific apathy,
to a heart felt surreal panorama of genuine concern for your fellow man.
You have not the ability to change your own love but the spirit is growing.
Your material being is transforming into an extension of hopefulness.

There is a ripple effect now and your love is spreading around and around.
That great lake of humanity is holding out open arms, giving you a crown.
Many souls are welcoming you into that eternal spirit of peacefulness.
You have now found your soul and are living free, flying into happiness.

Entering into the spirit, we share in all of God's grace, within and without.
He is within us and we are within his presence, without guilt or pain, found.
Eternity has begun and to die is to merely pass into yet another form.
We have already been transformed into another vehicle that is newborn.

To God be the glory and we are in his presence even standing on the Earth.
Love comes from God and springs forth as lightning bolts from dark clouds.
Love changes time and time changes hearts that were broken and hurt.
This is the time of changing love, creating a soul from a voice in the crowd.

by Cliff Rhodes
08/21/2008

Do You Feel It?

Do you feel the rays of the sun shining down and burning my skin?
It feels so wonderful and makes the freckles on my arm even browner.
Wind blows through my short hair and the cool breeze is like kisses.
My face feels the sting of little pine needles high up on the trail now.

My horse is running and I barely have time to brush away the branches.
The smell is exotic and pine sap is all in the air along with jasmine.
She takes control of my fantasies and her movements were all planned.
I don't even care and I have memorized how she looked and it plays again.

The recordings are memorized movements and scenes and conversations.
I remember the exact words she said and the feelings bring me happiness.
My late night dreams are all about her and are almost a tangible reality.
Maybe we should not even see each other so that we keep the attraction.

Do you feel the same thing that I feel, the tempest, the thunder, the rain?
If we see each other, I am sure that I will fall apart and not be so cool.
My heart beating will give me away and I won't be able to speak sanely.
I feel it and it takes me away into a dream land of wishes and moodiness.

I am wondering if you will take my hand and lead this man away trembling.
Will you feel it too, or will you hide it and not even show that you care?
If we dance, I am sure there will be moonlight and stars shining in heaven.
When I hold you close to me, you will feel my heart and know I am happy.

The horse knows when someone else is near and he always tells me.
He has his own way with motions and a lively step and his ears are high.
Another rider approaches and from a distance I can see more than memory.
Her reality is there in front of me, filling my eyes and sets my mind to fly!

By chance we both took to the trails today and luck brings us together.
The sun is hot and I notice that she has drops of sweat that are on her skin.
She says that the sun feels good and asks me if I feel that today is hotter.
I tell her that I think it is another wonderful day to feel the sun and wind.

I turn my horse around and ride with her along the same trails I crossed.
We ride to the end of the mountain until the terrain dives into the gorge.
Stopping at the end of the trail, we tie up in pine trees to rest and pause.
We lay next to each other on brown straw and watch clouds take form.

I watch and observe every little movement she makes, recording the event.
My mind will play back the hours, minutes, and seconds late in the night.
Dreams are made of realities and this day was a special time that we spent.
Together, so close, I watched her every movement and looked into her eyes.

We mounted our horses and I rode with her all the way back to the lodge.
Along the way we felt the sun, smelled the pine, and saw the birds in flight.
As the sun was dipping low into the horizon, she said goodbye and stopped.
Looking into each other eyes, time stayed motionless as I breathed a sigh.

Do you feel it, the nearness, the yearning, the fantasy of her memory?
I know it was real because I recorded it in my mind, to play over and over.

by Cliff Rhodes
08/23/2008

Virtual Joy Escape

Breaking into another realm of reality,
brings feelings of joy and insanity.
She welcomes my new me with annoyance.
I sense that this virtual world is no toy.

It is the same in virtuality as in real life.
Life is a many sided prism with light inside.
Bouncing light is our actions and feelings.
We are what we make of our own reality.

Building upon our visions,, we grow.
Putting layers of new ideas upon mistakes,
we hesitate and try again as if we know.
We know now that it was to build a wasteland.

The world we live in is of our own making.
Building what we already know is just a repetition.
There is no difference in the great escape.
We dreamed of a new reality but found again,

...sameness, with a new name.

Look for the paradigm shift of the brain wave.
Your own vision is a virtual wonder, escaping you.

by Cliff Rhodes
09/06/2008

Moving Inside Love's Dreams

I am fulfilled inside love's dreams and moving alive and awake.
I see her near me and moving as a spirit and I make contact.
Touching and feeling and knowing in the most expressive way,
I am what I am and I don't try to avoid her eyes and her hand.

Gently I kiss her and she takes away her hand from my lips.
I look longingly at her spirit and I can feel her expressive kiss.
Her lips barely touch mine and I know why she has found me again.
Loneliness has consumed her until she reached out to want to live.

She is alive in me and I am alive in her even though we can't exist.
Two lovers not there, not flesh and blood, but we live in the mind.
How can spirit caress and ghostly apparitions feel real love within?
It is a visitation from a thousand miles away and not just a whim.

She is in such sad refrain and is almost crying out for love.
Yet, I cannot give her any love except what spirit has already given.
Time is the medicine for the heart that no flesh can fulfill.
Healing is the kindness that she seeks and not my kiss or my skin.

The taste of an endless spirit and an eternal fountain is needed.
This will quiet her yearning and her needful passion to feel.
It will spring up into a daily refreshing that will never die or dim.
That light of bliss will not die out or grow dim as long as I live.

I will bring her into memory and lift her into my mind of wanting.
Taking her into my arms will quiet her fears of lonely dreaming.
She will feel my need and know that I am in the same place inside.
We need each other to reach inside the other's happy mind.

From thousands of miles away, we see each other inside spirit, ...and love.

by Cliff Rhodes
09/22/2008

Love's Blue Monkey Laughs

Laughter rings in my ears as my dreams align with hers.
She is my source of happiness ever since our minds merged.
We found each other in blue landscape of Saturn's outer rings.
Space was just a dream until we escaped the Earth to sing.

Our voices raised in joy, brought tears to both our eyes.
We heard such harmony in that blue intonation of desire.
Rushing winds were not too shy to take away our bashfulness.
We clothed ourselves in delight and rhythms of soulfulness.

Monkeys of compassion danced among the giraffes of yearning.
Exasperated longings kept us searching for ways not hurting.
"I promise I won't ever hurt you," she said, still teasing me.
I said, "Please hurt me a little longer until the dream is real."

Saturn takes back rings from monkeys that laugh too long and loud.
But, I know this dream is real, until she cries real tears, I've found.
Her tears are so like mine, since we have no pain to confess.
Gladness brings tears of laughter to monkeys' eyes that jest.

Our love is not the normal love that lives and dies a slow death.
It springs forth into eternity and refreshes itself after a test.
Love's blue monkey laughs, loud and long, at such a great happiness.
She alone is wisdom, bringing new life, and not a moment of sadness.

by Cliff Rhodes
10/04/2008

Love's Green Meadows of Mars

Love found a green meadow of Mars.
She said Mars, but it was not that far.
It was right in our own back yard.

Our minds found a place to rest.
We are not fighting and have no regrets.
That means we have finally passed the test.

Red plains and dry dust are all I remember.
Memories of all our troubles still hurt.
We never put the emotion of our planet first.

We were never ever from the Earth, anyway.
Mars has always been our planet in this space.
It is barren and cold with not one hospitable place.

Where lives that green meadow of emotion so content?
Our planet of discontent has been our best friend.
We don't even want any form of love to win.

Yet, there is that meadow, right in our back yard.
So close, it lies there waiting, not so far.
It is the lovely green meadow of Mars.

Now, that star has risen again in our minds.
We dream that the light of love shines bright.
Our hearts have found forgiveness again this time.

Let your heart too hold fast love inside.
Keep safe that green meadow of your life.
Love will find the place that will not be denied.

Green meadows of memories live again on Mars.

by Cliff Rhodes
10/09/2008

Oh! Love's New Enigma

Love is at my door and she wants to talk this time.
She has been waiting since the dawn and will not relent.
I am fading in and out of my reality and cannot say why.
I don't know if the breath I breathe is from spirit or within.

"Hello love, and I have to say your name again, Love."
You are still the same mystery, yet the same one I trust.
How can mystery of mysteries be so coy and funny?
Lo, we look here and lo, we look there but not above.

Then suddenly, wings are around us and we only struggle.
Tied up in knots, we are and no way to move, not a little.
She smiles because spirit has moved and won again my love.
I only deserve to die but I am alive and I smile back, quickly.

I am not what you think I am and not a bit bashful either.
Oh! Love's new enigma has broken and lies in pieces.
She laughs as gently as the breeze when I touch her hand.
"Not a word, don't breathe a word", she says, so fantastic.

The bell chimes and I look around, wondering where I am.
I can't remember this place because it is entirely new.
Her dress is completely red and made of velvety fabric.
There has been a paradigm shift and I am in her bedroom.

Time and space have moved, just a little, inside a golden orb.
We are caught in the shift and grab each other's hand.
Fast and instantaneous is the moving spirit that takes form.
We are in a moonbow with colors muted as we begin to dance.

by Cliff Rhodes
10/20/2008

What Is Love's Question?

Love, Oh Love, you ask me that question over and over again.

But what is the nature of the problem this time, at this place?

You know that I cannot tell one from the other and will never win.

How many days have been lost and how many hearts yet to break?

We deny our existence and we say that we were never to be together.

Long days and nights I stay awake and wonder how you will react.

I cannot keep this charade up much longer, but surely not forever.

I will not hide my love inside this crystal skull with light fading fast.

Ask of me your enchanting question and I will explain so gladly.

Only you and I will know the answer that comes from my lips.

It will not wait but a moment and time will release it as you planned.

My answer will be forthcoming as fast as the dove lifts her wings.

When the dew is upon the grass in the morning we know of change.

As the sun dries up the water from the tender leaves, we see sorrow.

Only for a moment was there water to drink as with only a drop of rain.

Love is here inside my heart and I feel warmth, but what of tomorrow?

Your question is rolling round and round in my head but I cannot think.

My answer is not allowed to proceed from my lips, yet I breathe.

Were I able to fly up into the clouds I would take you with me.

Away we would float upon the winds, and sail the ocean but never sink.

Take this fruit, my love, and let it steal away your desire for another.

Let the light of my blue eyes be as the sun upon the dew in the morning.

Hold my hand and let it be warmth to you again as the sun dries your tears.

Let my strong legs support you as I cuddle you in my arms and take form.

What question could possibly be asked if you already know the answer?

by Cliff Rhodes

10/27/2008

After the Election, Liberty and Love Still Reign Supreme

Liberty and Love are still the same, even after an election.
Freedom speaks of less coercion and less government.
We know who has decided our own fate and it was us.
There will be more of one and less of another to repent.

We will all regret that it was not enough to just be truthful.
Should we have fought more bitterly and been more decisive?
Maybe there could be a different outcome if we were resentful.
Doubting this we can only say that God will be more vindictive.

We were not very persuasive, defending innocents, but He will be.
God judged the people for sacrificing hundreds to idol Molech.
Who could believe that he will not remember billions of babies?
As above so below, God will appear, even in dark heaven.

Love and Freedom are the same and one cannot live alone.
One either vanishes or finds a different place to thrive together.
Where love of these little ones is no more, then freedom goes.
America is not long for the pile of bones that speaks of death.

When babies are not safe, then those in power have no respect.
Who will take their orders, and who will look into their eyes?
All will avoid our leaders for fear of what will befall them.
Love and Freedom, together, make bold the words of the wise.

But the words of those quick to do evil will fly away with the wind.
Yes we can, yes we can, yes we can have liberty without love.
They think they can take away the breath of the innocent without
responsibility.
Tears shed in victory are hollow indeed and appear like acid rain
against the sin.

Fight with me, fight with me, fight with me against taxation and oppression.
The heels are on and the gloves are off, but her courage alone was not enough.
It was not enough to know the truth because an illusion of freedom was too great.
With liberty comes responsibility and self sacrifice to win the race.

"Suffer little children and forbid them not to come unto me," said Christ.
"There is none good, but one, that is God," he said again.
For four years we will hold our breath while many breaths are taken away.
Liberty without love has no conscience and cannot breathe in freedom alive.

After the election, Liberty and Love still reign supreme, except in America.
There is Liberty and there is Love but they are dying a slow death, being separated from each other.

by Cliff Rhodes
11/10/2008

We Are Traveling Through The Milky Way Galaxy

The location of our solar system in the spiral of The Milky Way Galaxy brings phenomena paranormal.

We will now begin finding new solutions to problems that have plagued us to resolve before. In times past it was amusing that President George Bush made slips that were repeated over and over continuously in late night talk show pointless entertainment.

The problem now is that writers have an immediate void in fodder for comedians. They can't make fun of Barack Obama, because the Democratic Party controls the media. Not that there probably will of course certainly be slip ups when he takes office but it will be a non subject because of the strangle hold the liberals have on the media.

Talk show hosts will not be allowed to have political humor unless it is old Bush stuff, which will of necessity be reruns, repeats, and rehashed funny lines that Republicans made in the past, so boring. No new stuff will surface and suddenly political humor will just cease to exist any more. That is going to really be bizarre.

What else could possibly be made fun of, except us, the public. We will now be the brunt of jokes, the taxpayers, being had by the government. That will really be funny. The economy will survive but only after beneficial sums of our own money have been throttled into companies who have deeply embedded lobbyists in congress. It has already started with AIG execs. taking spa vacations on our newest bailout. The newly elected President and incoming congress will be hands off for the liberal controlled media.
The other point in being at a different place in the Milky Way Galaxy is the tragic aspect of the joke. God will certainly be getting his revenge against those who have been oppressively and horrendously taking the lives of the unborn. The act of betrayal to humanity by those trying to stand on the pitiful civil liberties rights to choose death for their unborn infant because of simple inconvenience will now become a flash point.

162

Those mysterious new bands of electromagnetic radiation that we are beginning to pass through will certainly and hopefully stir the consciousness of patriots spread across the United States who feel that their souls have finally been sadly offended by the millions of useless deaths.

The real punch line to this tragedy is what will our own punishment be for allowing such a liberal socialist to be elected in the first place? We didn't try hard enough to get out the vote so we alone are ultimately responsible and will suffer our own just rewards. We can't blame anybody but ourselves. Someone told me once that the greatest sin is the sin of omission, the sin of what you could have but didn't do.

So thusly we will all suffer for our own inability to convince others of the impending doom of a socialist administration. The question is whether or not we will be able to tell a Democratic Party Socialist from a Republican Party Socialist since they blend together so evenly and transition so smoothly.

Barack Obama and John McCain were almost holding hands when the 700 billion dollar bailout was begged and cajoled out of Congress. There is a list of the billions that each busted bank received on the internet but they don't really have to tell you how they spent the money.

Does anybody really believe that if it was put on the ballot and brought before the voters of this country, to borrow money from China, that it would pass? Of course not and neither would any bailout pass a voter test for banks or mortgage companies or insurance companies and not even auto manufacturers. It has to be shuffled through congress where all the lobbyists have set up camp.

What kind of democracy are we really living in anyway?

The answer is one with funny money, leaders with no conscience, and a vengeful God who loves us enough to chastise us for our own mistakes.

by Cliff Rhodes   11/13/2008

An Orb Travels Across The Matrix, Drawing Love

Those who had lost hope within hope still yearned for something better.
They thought they had found it in this new promise but now they wonder.
He seems like a great electrifier of inspiration and a hope to the hopeless.
What they don't know is that he is drying up their means of redress.

Every dream is not a nightmare and every sweet dream is not heaven sent.
The fundamental principles of the ground upon which they stand is rotten.
Decay is the forecast for he who doesn't insure the survival of the weakest.
His constituents remember promises made and will receive full payment.

An orb travels across the matrix of humanity and draws love from hope.
Misplaced admiration does not give solace to the innocent lives lost alone.
Redress of grievances doesn't fit crimes done so long ago in ancient history.
Speeches about making changes to insure greater benefits are tired irony.

Character cannot be entitled or insured or legislated to benefit the poor.
Those who float within a cesspool of money are already poorly scorned.
They build their houses upon the idea that it is better to obfuscate a lie.
Continue the sophistry, perpetuate discrimination tomes, don't let it die.

Now, we wait not upon the outcome of what will surely eventually appear.
It can only be the evidence of the continuation of the same, over and over.
How can bad character continue to spiral downward in a circular pattern?
Because, it is fed and nurtured, loved and aspired to in the upbeat world.

Hidden among the celebrations are the small almost invisible beings.
They don't cry out because they have not fully formed but still electrify.
Within their world are strings of electrical, spiritual forms with wings.
They don't feel except to exist and that is their crime that we must dignify.

What redress will be given to them when all of their spirit combines?
They cannot speak for themselves or lobby for a bailout to congress.
That is too bad for the oppressors since God will surely intervene instead.
He will invade without mercy the ground upon which they have died!

Let us seek God's mercy for the wrongs that we have made in derision.
We should pray for our country that it will really change directions.
All of us are guilty of the sins of omission because we have failed.
We have failed to save the unborn, those who are weakest and truly hated.

by Cliff Rhodes
11/25/2008

Grateful for Love of Friends and Family

Grateful for the love of friends and family, I think about a premonition.
We see emblazoned upon tv screens the horror of torment and terror.
Like a movie trailer of something yet to come are bombs and bullets again.
The whole world is their stage upon which to practice and perfectly burn.

Always they proceed to one country or another with death and destruction.
Leaving one and returning again to another, they report back their deeds.
Don't they know that God and mankind hear the echoes within confusion?
With glee they think that a blackened smudge of smoke will succeed.

Bullets and bombs will not overshadow the mesmerizing attraction of love.
Our constitution of sharp spring steel will cut clean through, forever.
Divide our families if you will or burn our cities, yet God prevails above.
How it must sting, that sharp pain of regret and depression, with failure.

To know and to realize that nothing will prevail against love, must be sad.
Blessings we have and honor and time to mend and grow stronger still.
So what damage has been done to spirit or to soul that speaks as crystal?
Seeing on through, into the depths of consciousness, sets us free at last.

We will not disseminate or disperse and we will not slow our steps aright.
Boldly we set our path of righteousness, framed from Biblical ideals.
The shadow created by the light of reason permeates even the darkest sky.
We see your silhouettes clearly as ashes of your bones upon a green tree.

Even though we know that we are dead there still lives another yet still.
The next one and then the next one will know of love and all its happiness.
Spirit never even slows down or diverts from reason or truth to win.
Try as they may to terrorize, we humbly express to God our gratefulness.

by Cliff Rhodes
11/27/2008

Flash of Bright Light, Love Leads Onward

Flash of staccato images in rapid succession dominates vision.
Love is around and inside and melting hearts of stone and sinew.
How many paths has love shown us to travel, we of indecision?
Must we continue to ignore and only assume that failure looms?

Rapid fire progression of spirit touching minds and hearts burn.
Aching hearts yearn for new direction, doubting self again hurts.
We are standing on the sidelines and wishing to get in the game.
Holding back our intentions, showing nonchalant, we are afraid.

How could God pick us to speak without fear, without hatred?
Roaring in my ears is not a voice I am hearing, but a whisper.
It encourages me to speak what is on my mind and tell the tale.
It is a story about the courage of others, like myself who resist.

They have read the proverbs and history of men who have failed.
They do not wish to take their ship into shoals of heavy fishes.
They know that their own mistakes will make them deathly afraid.
But they will take that step with abandon and trust in the spirit.

How many swords have you, only two? Then it is enough, go on.
You will not need even one, but let it be like a truck full of gold.
How much can you carry with you from place to place, a ton?
They have thousands, yet you may get insight when the ear goes.

When you cannot hear yourself speak but another, turn to the ear.
God gave you two ears and one mouth so why act like the deaf?
Love is all around you and even murderers love themselves.
They are afraid of what they have done and always fear death.

Flash of bright light, spirit grabs and pulls at hearts today.
Tugging and fighting, suddenly they give up their sins willingly.
He has spoken from a void and from the abyss of sudden decay.
Stretching out their hands, they plead innocently for reprieve.

Horror of horrors the time has come all too soon and I am sad.
What, now is the time and not later? But I thought I had time.
No! It is now and time waits not for those who never plan.
Prepare your soul, for the time comes not later, but arrives.

Flash of bright light, loves leads onward to distant shores.
Some may think that they are immune from the test of time.
God may judge today or may judge tomorrow and take form.
Tarry not at insignificant things but buried in repentance, baptized.

by Cliff Rhodes
11/29/2008

Love Is Not A Mirror, But A Wave

Love spreads out in concentric circles and ricochets, one on one.
Love is not a mirror that bounces light back and forth, just to you.
Love may not return to you again and again or always be such fun.
Love is a wave that radiates out, making life completely new.

Sadness is such a short episode in life that loves even fear and stress.
These are only tools by which to make us stronger and also wiser.
Every person has the same vindication for all of life's duration test.
All of us in this world deserve love and that is why love is so alive.

Love waits for you, and love knows you, and love invites you to live.
Strive to enable your spirit to extend your loving nature to succeed.
Love is a machine, never tiring to encourage, and making friends.
Circle upon circle, the vortex of enchantment spirals out into reality.

Love is not a dream, not just imagination, and especially not false
hope.
Love does not tread lightly upon lies and deceit or abuse and
oppression.
There is justice in love, because love is so hopeful and overpowering.
Truth is the dedication of spirit to love and never leaves truth alone.

Liberty still sings love's praises, yet travels a difficult path today.
She knows that truth is her guardian and hope is her shaft of light.
Those who try to tear down her fortress will end in dismal decay.
Freedom takes love's hand and together they fly to win the mind.

by Cliff Rhodes
12/11/2008

www.ingramcontent.com/pod-product-compliance
Lightning Source LLC
Chambersburg PA
CBHW021233090426
42740CB00006B/512